Ocean Adventures

STORY-TIME TREASURY

Table of Contents

Dolphin

by Kathleen Weidner Zoehfeld
Illustrated by Steven James Petruccio

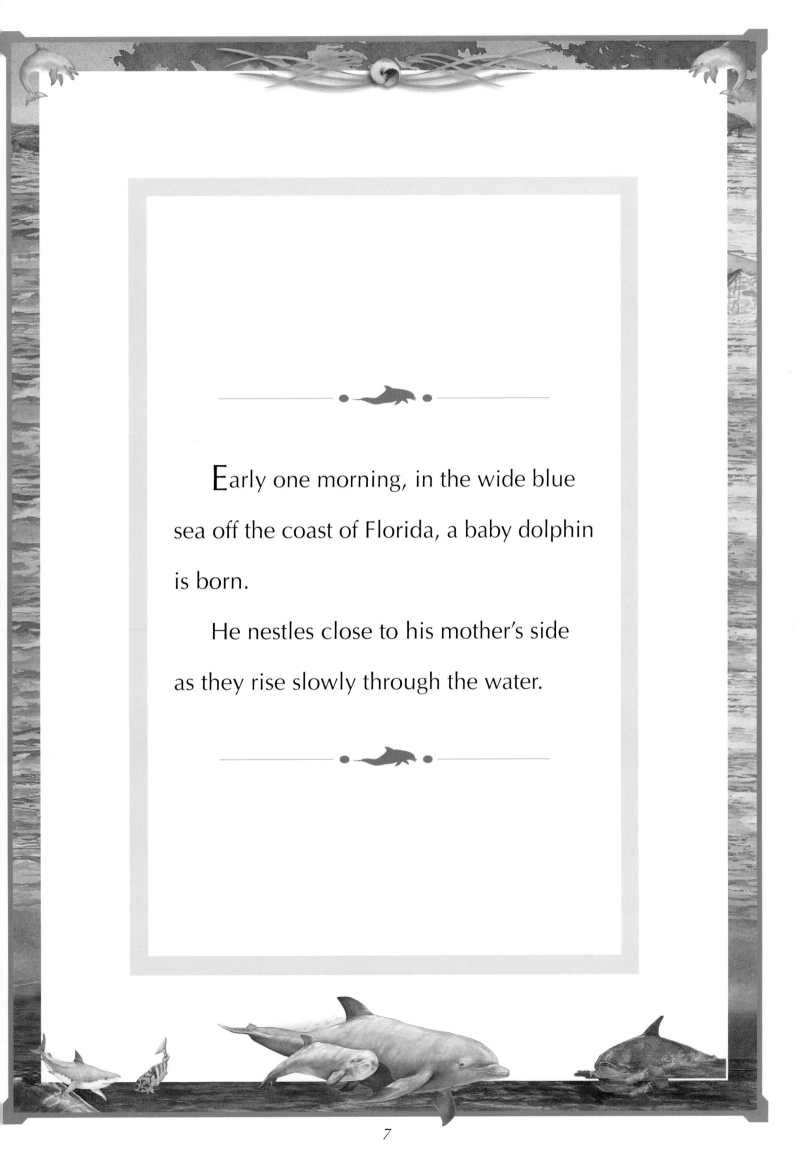

Early one morning, in the wide blue sea off the coast of Florida, a baby dolphin is born.

He nestles close to his mother's side as they rise slowly through the water.

Another dolphin swims nearby. She strokes the little calf with her flipper. She will be Little Dolphin's nanny.

Little Dolphin feels his mother and nanny nudging him up through the water. They reach the surface and Little Dolphin feels cool air on his back.

Pfoosh! He opens his blowhole and takes his first breath.

Little Dolphin peeks out above the water. The ocean sparkles like melted gold all around him. The sun is a golden fire in the deep blue sky.

The morning air is quiet. But below, the ocean is alive with sounds—the pops of snapping shrimp, the distant croaks and creaks of pilot whales, the grunts and squeaks of a thousand different fishes.

Little Dolphin and his mother travel with six other dolphins. The group swims slowly so that Little Dolphin and his mother can rest and nurse.

Little Dolphin is messy when he drinks his mother's milk. He spills everywhere! The milk makes him feel strong and frisky. Soon he will swim as well as his mother.

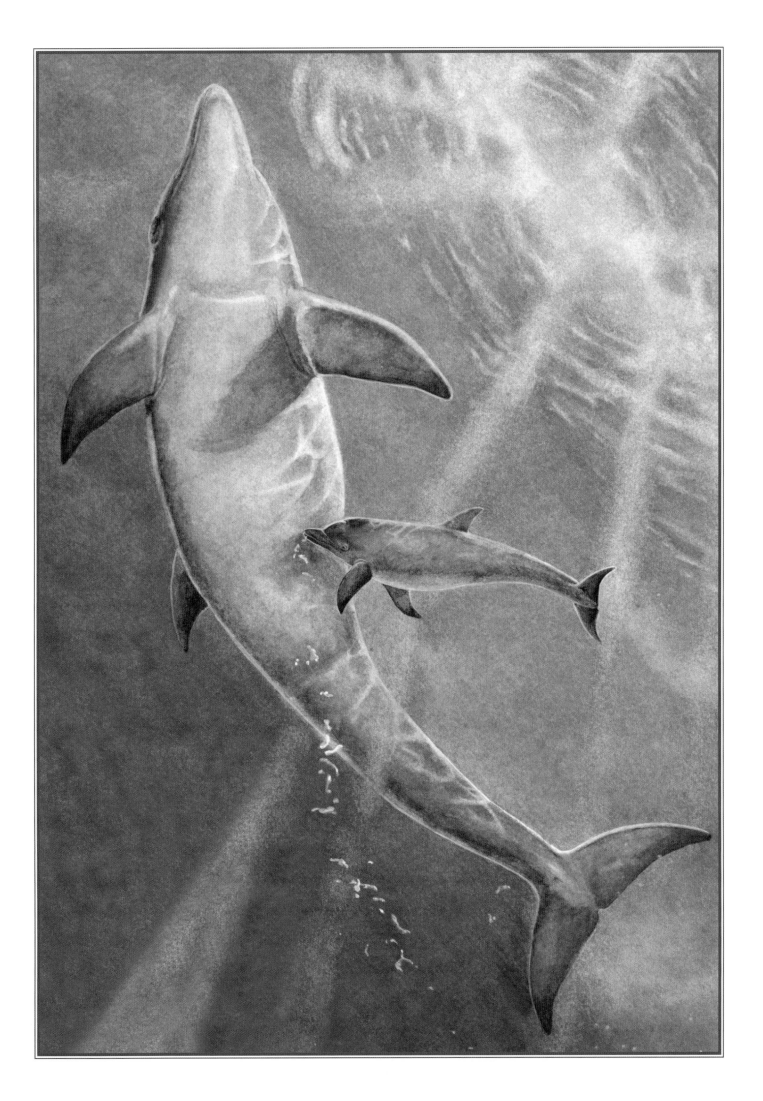

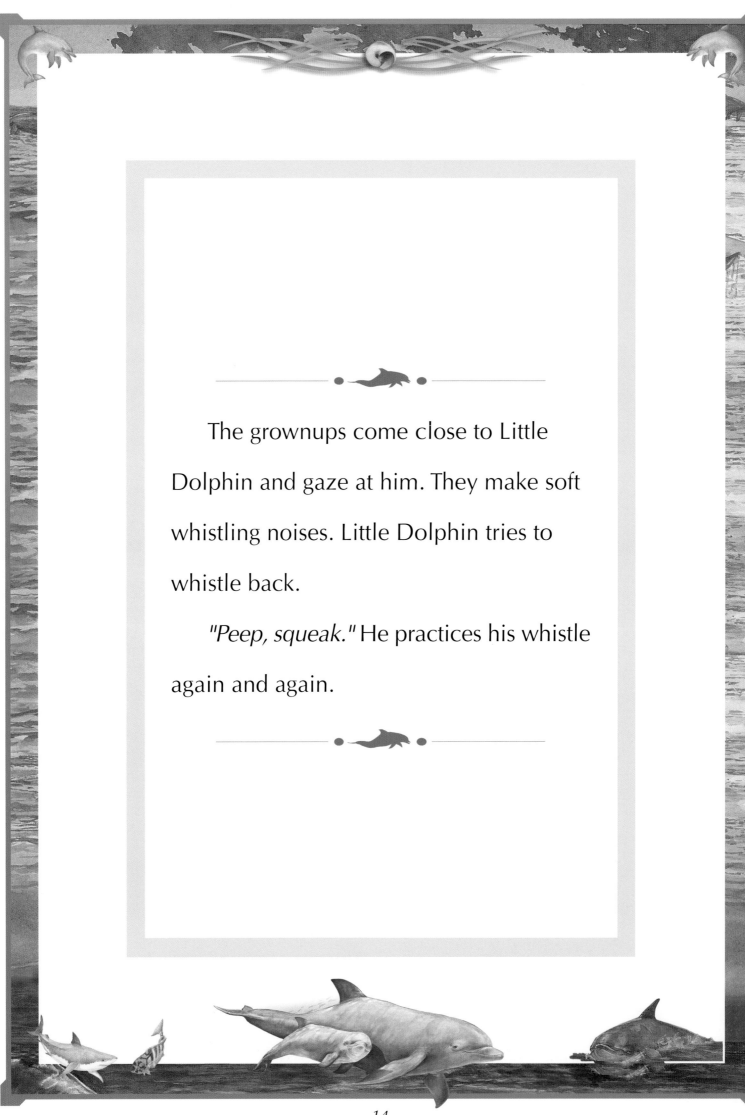

The grownups come close to Little Dolphin and gaze at him. They make soft whistling noises. Little Dolphin tries to whistle back.

"Peep, squeak." He practices his whistle again and again.

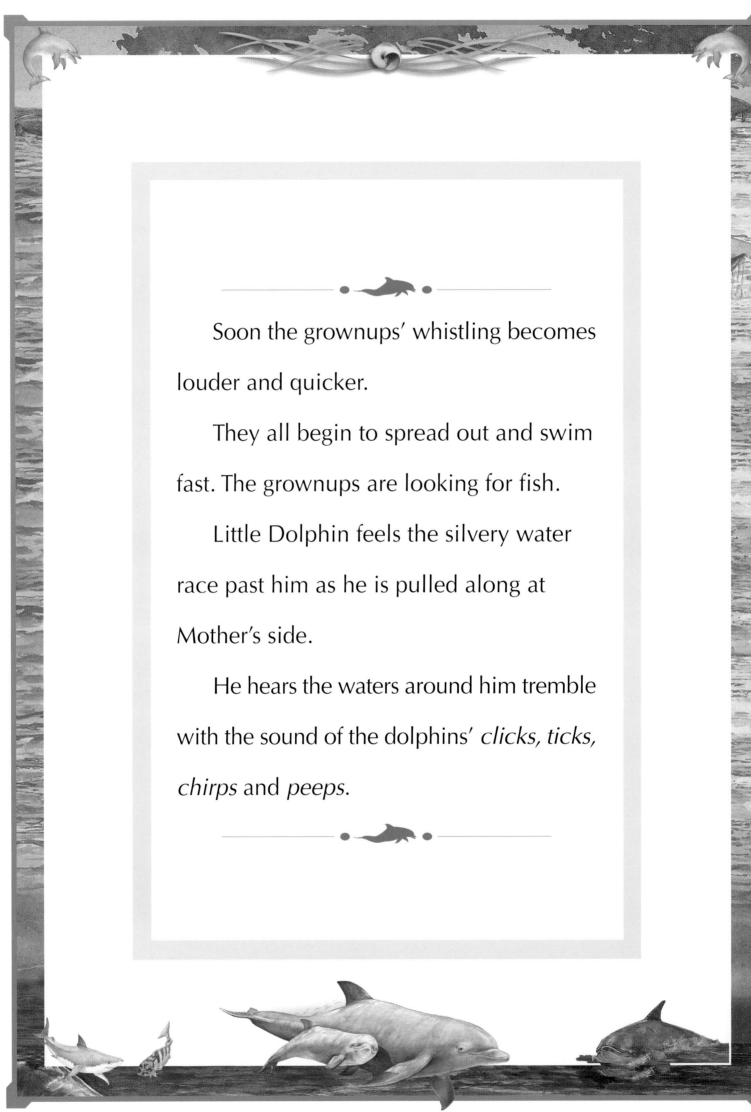

Soon the grownups' whistling becomes louder and quicker.

They all begin to spread out and swim fast. The grownups are looking for fish.

Little Dolphin feels the silvery water race past him as he is pulled along at Mother's side.

He hears the waters around him tremble with the sound of the dolphins' *clicks, ticks, chirps* and *peeps.*

The clicking sounds speed through the water ahead of the dolphins. Before long they hear echoes of their own sharp whistles, as the sounds bounce off hundreds of small moving shapes in the water.

By listening to the echoes, the dolphins know that a school of fish is up ahead. They charge in closer.

Little Dolphin's mother uses her snout to fling a fish high in the air. It lands on the water with a smack. The fish makes a tasty meal.

The air above fills with the swoosh of pelican wings and the squawk of hungry gulls.

The birds dive at the surface of the water, stealing the fish the dolphins leave behind.

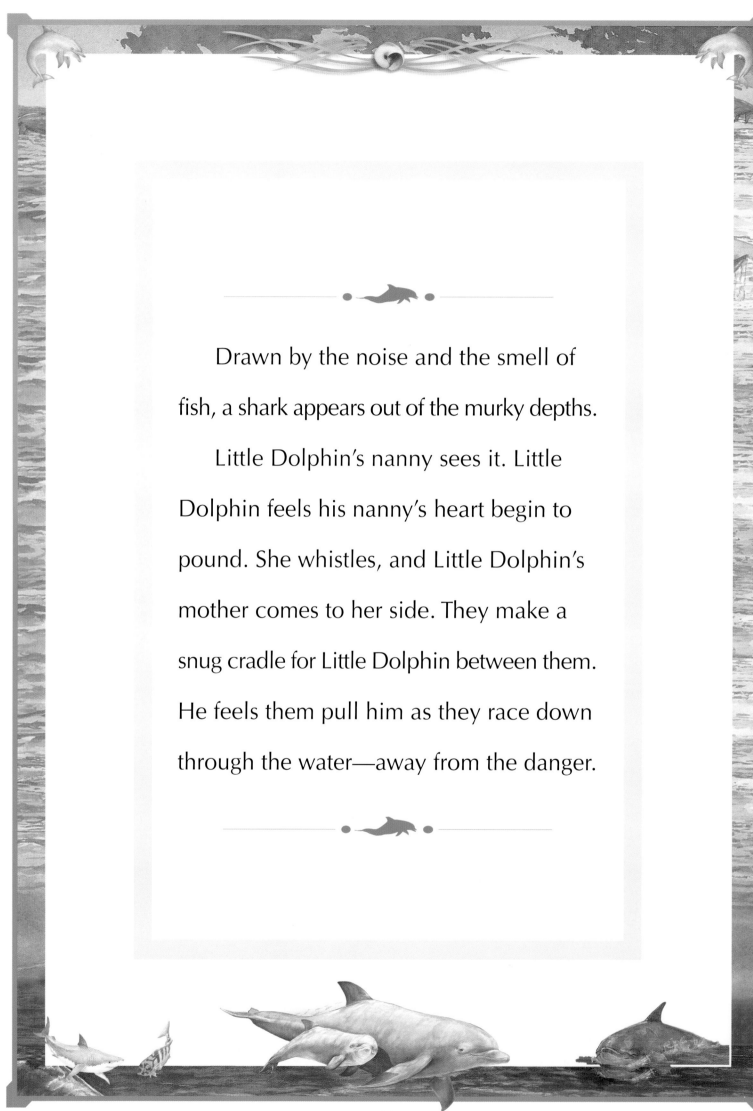

Drawn by the noise and the smell of
fish, a shark appears out of the murky depths.
Little Dolphin's nanny sees it. Little
Dolphin feels his nanny's heart begin to
pound. She whistles, and Little Dolphin's
mother comes to her side. They make a
snug cradle for Little Dolphin between them.
He feels them pull him as they race down
through the water—away from the danger.

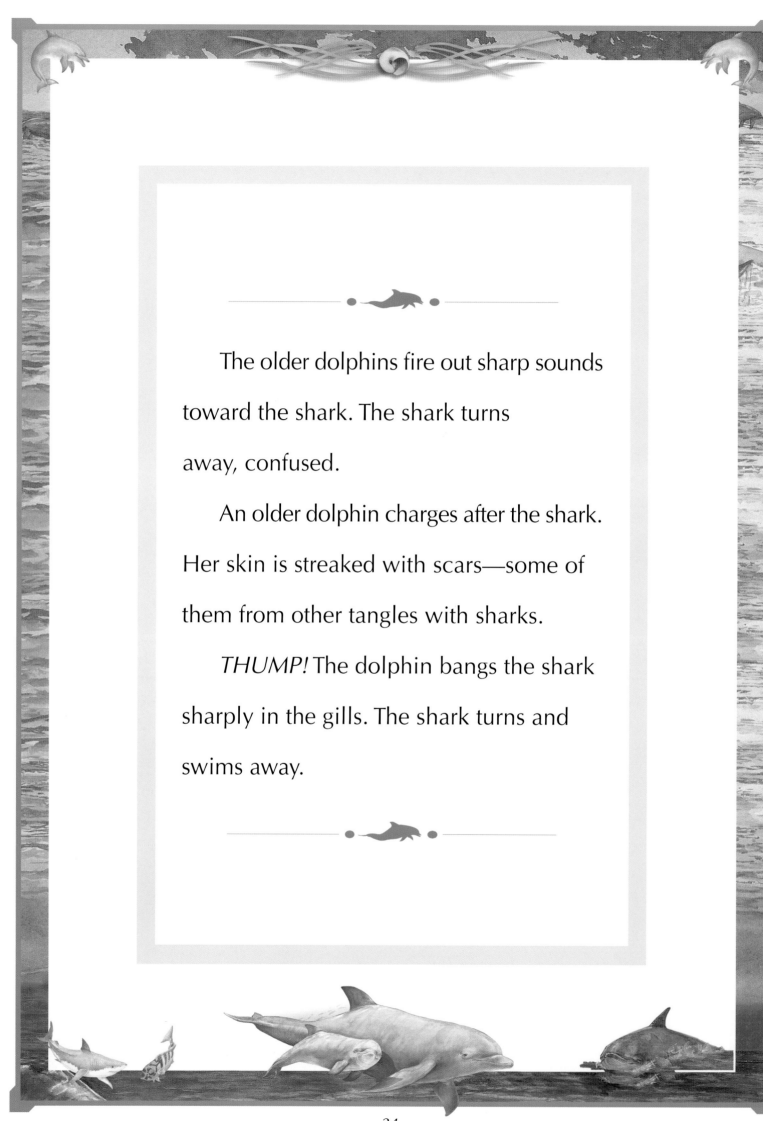

The older dolphins fire out sharp sounds toward the shark. The shark turns away, confused.

An older dolphin charges after the shark. Her skin is streaked with scars—some of them from other tangles with sharks.

THUMP! The dolphin bangs the shark sharply in the gills. The shark turns and swims away.

Little Dolphin and his mother and nanny return to the surface. Dolphins from another pod arrive. Some of the grownups dive down and circle around one another. They leap high out of the water. Little Dolphin watches. He hears them whistle and chatter.

Two older babies swim over and offer Little Dolphin a piece of seaweed. They push it back and forth as if it were a little toy.

As the sun settles down near the horizon, the other dolphins begin to go their separate ways. Little Dolphin snuggles against his mother's side.

Above, the evening sky darkens until it matches the deep blue of the ocean. Mother whistles softly to her new baby. The waves rock them back and forth, and soon Little Dolphin is asleep.

Blue Crab

by Kathleen Hollenbeck
Illustrated by Joanie Popeo

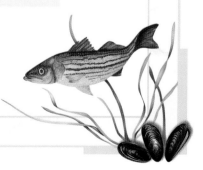

It is a bright morning and sunlight sparkles on the waters of the bay. Gentle waves lap the shore, leaving a trail of white foam along the water's edge.

Beneath the shallow water, Blue Crab scuttles sideways on the sand.

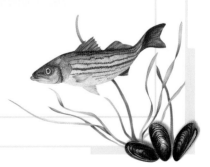

Crack! Crack! Blue Crab spies two male crabs fighting nearby. Their claws are locked together. Each waits for the right moment to make the next move. Suddenly, they struggle! One of the crabs is injured and hurries away. The winner scuttles off in the opposite direction in search of food.

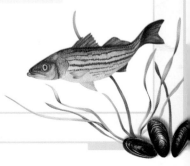

Something moves behind Blue Crab.
She turns to see a male crab standing high
on his three pairs of walking legs. The male
crab knows that Blue Crab is watching.
He stretches his claws straight out on each
side and lifts his hind pair of legs up behind
him. These legs are shaped like paddles and
he waves them quickly from side to side.
He is dancing for Blue Crab.

Soon it will be time for Blue Crab to shed her old shell and grow a new, larger one. She has cast off her shell, or molted, many times before. But this time is special. This time Blue Crab will become an adult, able to make eggs. She will need a male crab to protect her and to mate with her.

Joining the dance, Blue Crab waves her claws quickly from side to side and scuttles closer.

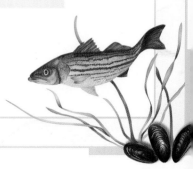

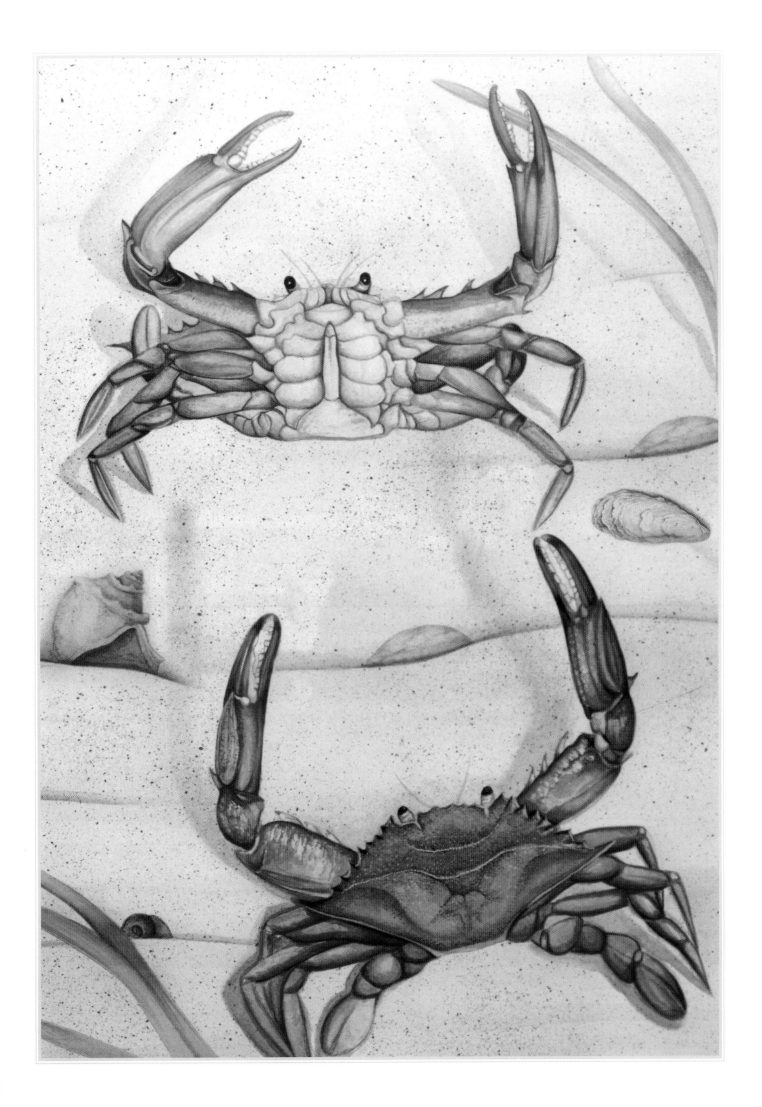

Blue Crab folds in her claws and the male crab wraps his six walking legs around her. He swims with his paddles, carrying Blue Crab to a safe hiding spot where she can molt.

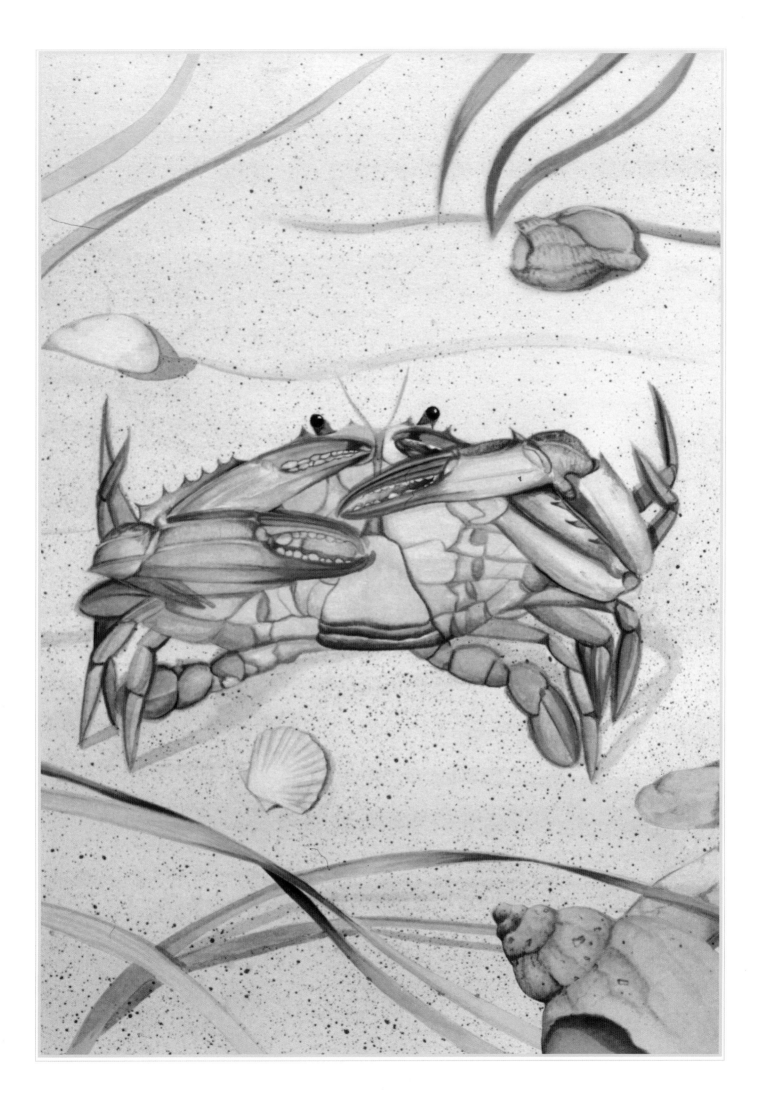

Blue Crab's mate chooses a hollow spot next to a large clump of eel grass. He stands high, making a protective cage around Blue Crab with his legs. Blue Crab's shell splits. It is time for her to molt.

For the next few hours, Blue Crab works with all her might. Little by little she pulls her soft body out of the old hard shell.

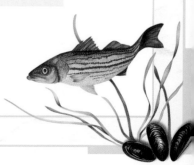

The male crab stands guard while Blue Crab rests. Her new shell is paper-soft and will take several days to harden. Blue Crab's mate carries her as before, keeping her safe while her soft shell grows hard and strong.

In early fall, it is time for Blue Crab to leave her mate and move south. Her eggs will need the warmer, saltier water found there.

Close to shore one day, Blue Crab senses danger. A great blue heron stretches its neck toward Blue Crab and stabs the water with its long, sharp beak. Blue Crab jumps back and burrows into the mud. She stays there until the heron is gone.

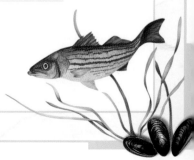

When spring arrives, Blue Crab has completed her journey. Now, about two million tiny eggs cling in clusters to Blue Crab's abdomen, or apron.

While her eggs develop, Blue Crab hunts for food. One afternoon, she seizes something tasty with her claw. It tugs back and drags Blue Crab up out of the water. Blue Crab has been caught! She hangs from a piece of bait at the end of a string. Her eggs glisten in the sunlight.

The string jerks sharply. Blue Crab lets go of the bait and falls into a pail held by human hands. Suddenly the pail overturns, sending Blue Crab plunging back into the water. She lands on the bottom and scuttles quickly away, leaving a muddy cloud behind her.

Blue Crab cannot know that because she is carrying eggs, the crabber set her free.

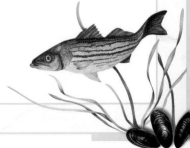

Finally, Blue Crab's eggs hatch in the warm, salty ocean. They drift off, teeny tiny creatures floating through the water. They will continue to molt and grow into blue crabs like their parents.

On her own again, Blue Crab will spend her days traveling beneath the sparkling waters.

Sea Otter

by Doe Boyle
Illustrated by Robert Lawson

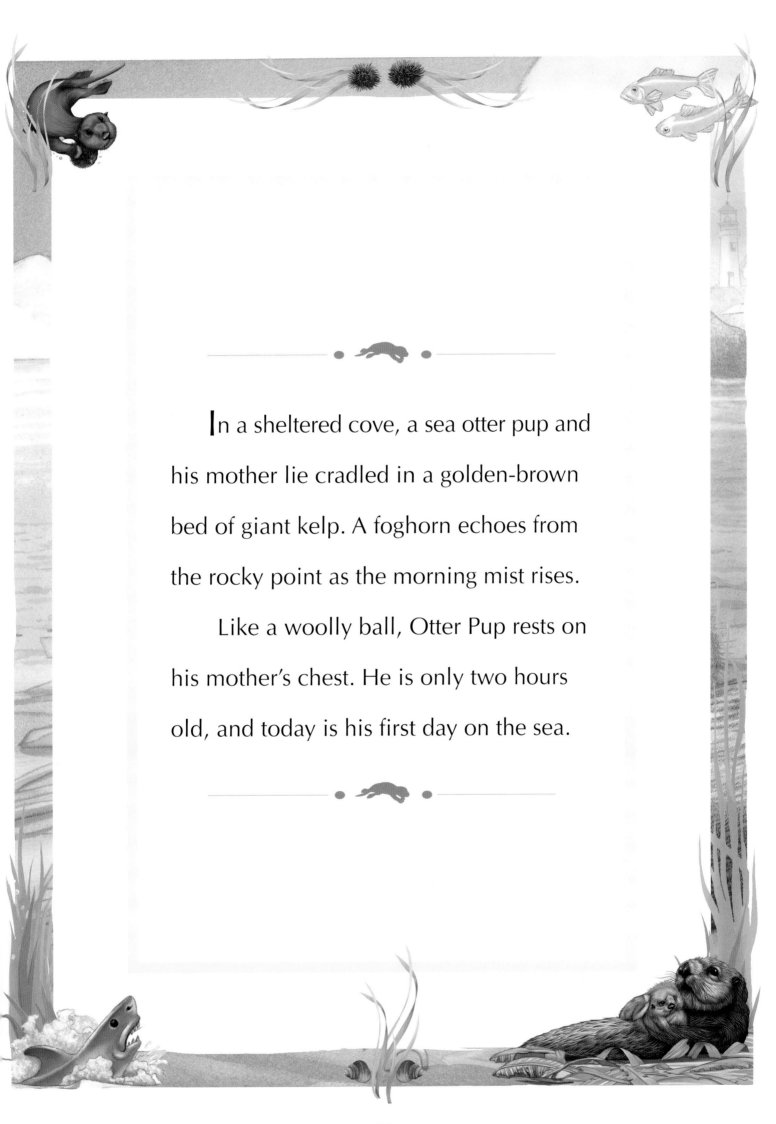

In a sheltered cove, a sea otter pup and his mother lie cradled in a golden-brown bed of giant kelp. A foghorn echoes from the rocky point as the morning mist rises.

Like a woolly ball, Otter Pup rests on his mother's chest. He is only two hours old, and today is his first day on the sea.

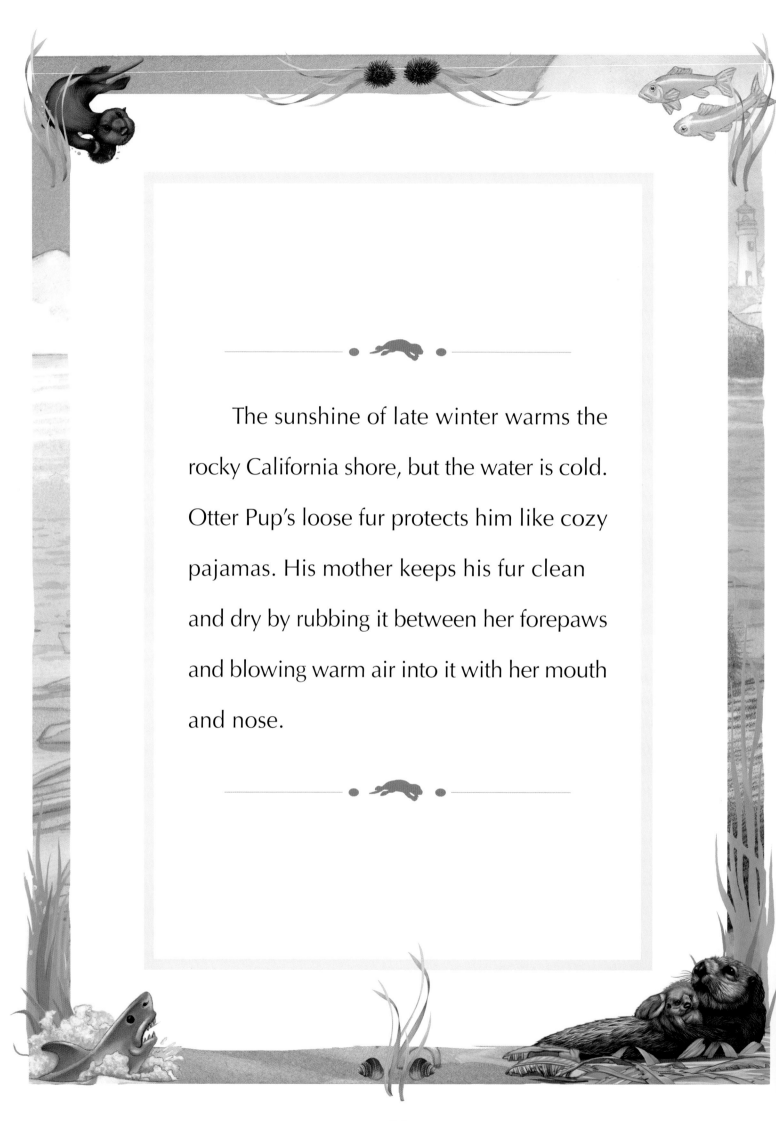

The sunshine of late winter warms the rocky California shore, but the water is cold. Otter Pup's loose fur protects him like cozy pajamas. His mother keeps his fur clean and dry by rubbing it between her forepaws and blowing warm air into it with her mouth and nose.

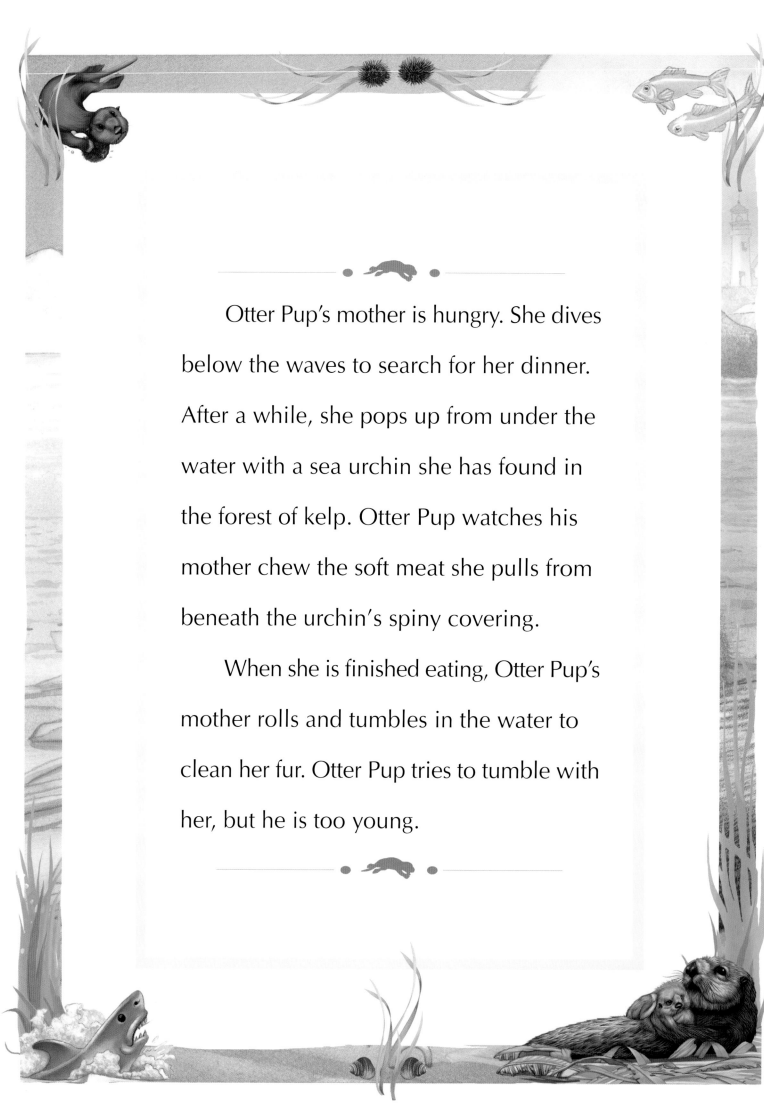

Otter Pup's mother is hungry. She dives below the waves to search for her dinner. After a while, she pops up from under the water with a sea urchin she has found in the forest of kelp. Otter Pup watches his mother chew the soft meat she pulls from beneath the urchin's spiny covering.

When she is finished eating, Otter Pup's mother rolls and tumbles in the water to clean her fur. Otter Pup tries to tumble with her, but he is too young.

For several months, Otter Pup shares his mother's food. Otter Pup's mother breaks the hard shells of clams and abalone with rocks she finds on the ocean floor.

Crack! Crack! The sound of her pounding carries above the cries of the seagulls who wait to steal fallen morsels.

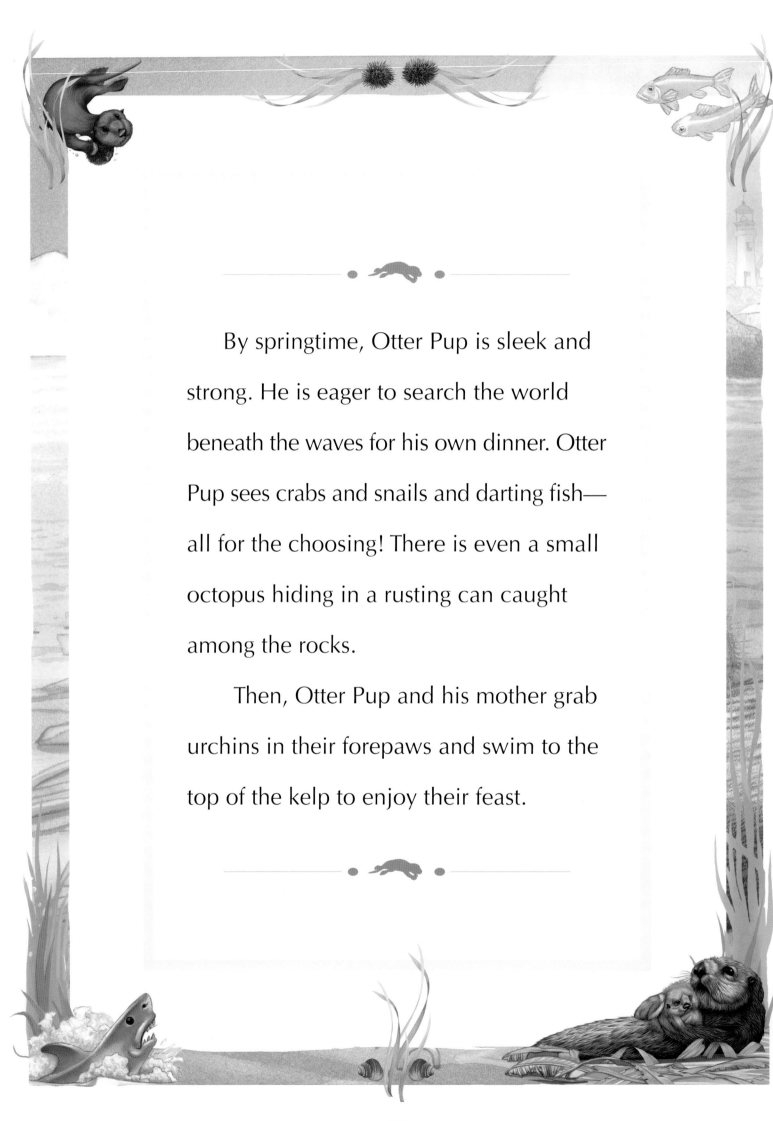

By springtime, Otter Pup is sleek and strong. He is eager to search the world beneath the waves for his own dinner. Otter Pup sees crabs and snails and darting fish—all for the choosing! There is even a small octopus hiding in a rusting can caught among the rocks.

Then, Otter Pup and his mother grab urchins in their forepaws and swim to the top of the kelp to enjoy their feast.

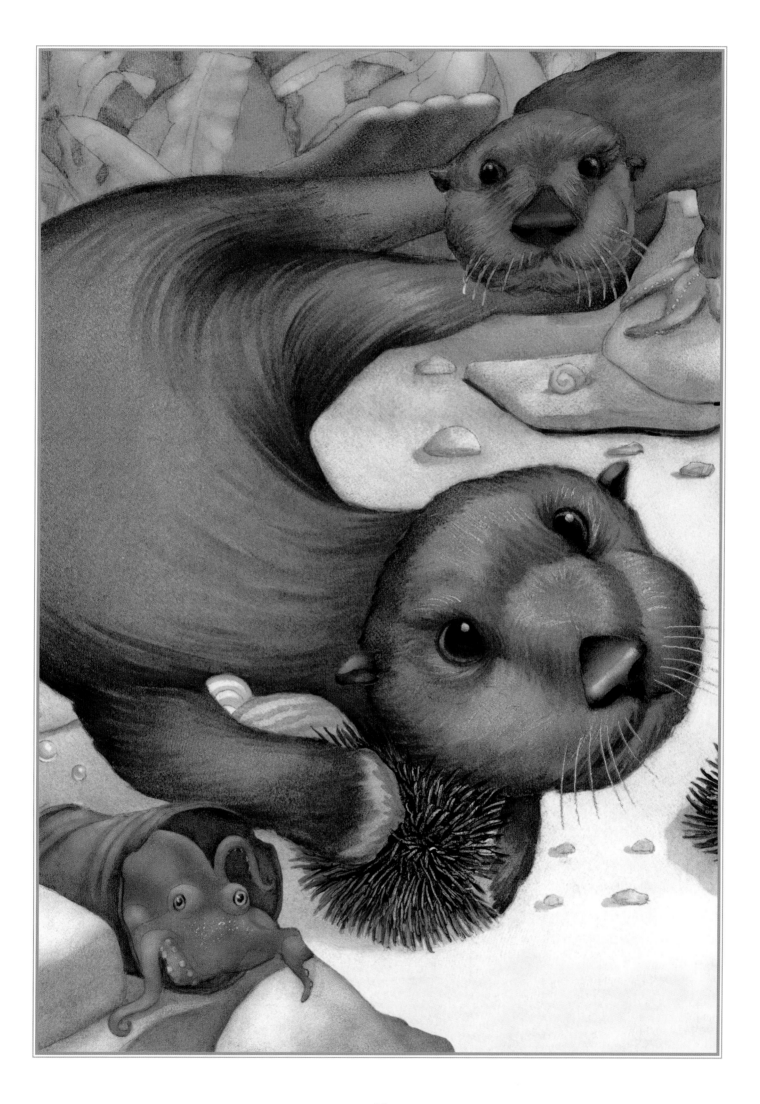

Floating on his back, Otter Pup spreads his dinner on his belly and tears at an urchin. He snorts and sniffs, eating the treasures he has found below.

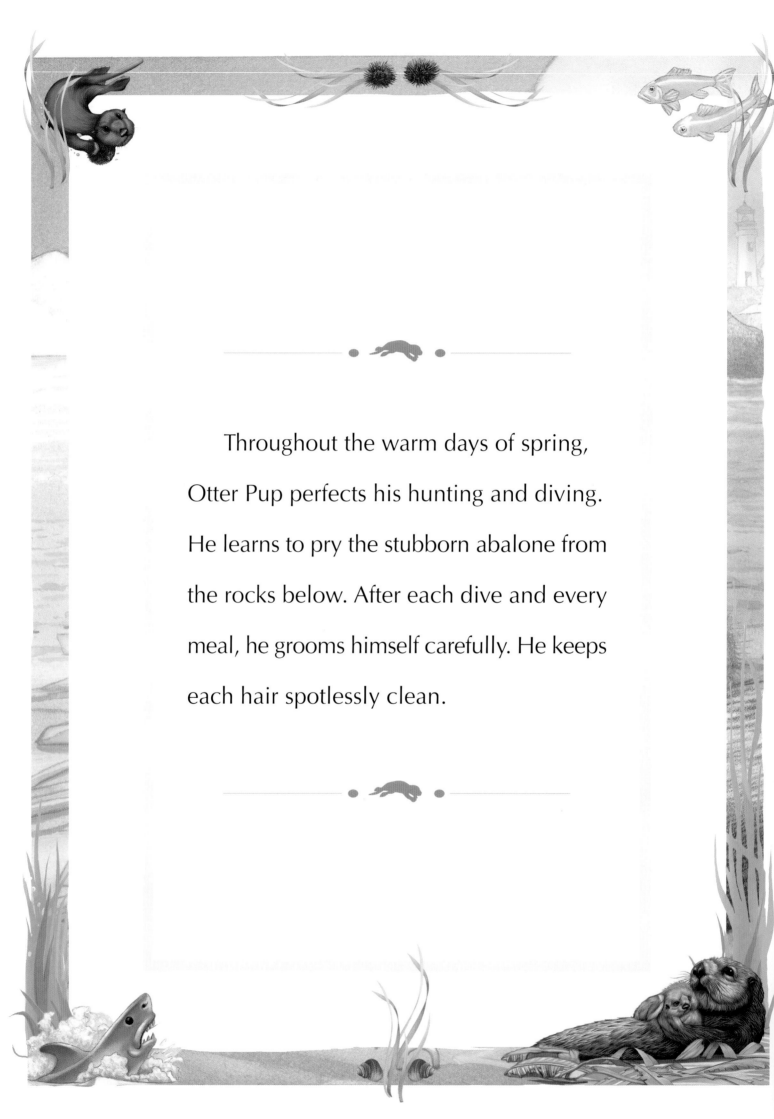

Throughout the warm days of spring, Otter Pup perfects his hunting and diving. He learns to pry the stubborn abalone from the rocks below. After each dive and every meal, he grooms himself carefully. He keeps each hair spotlessly clean.

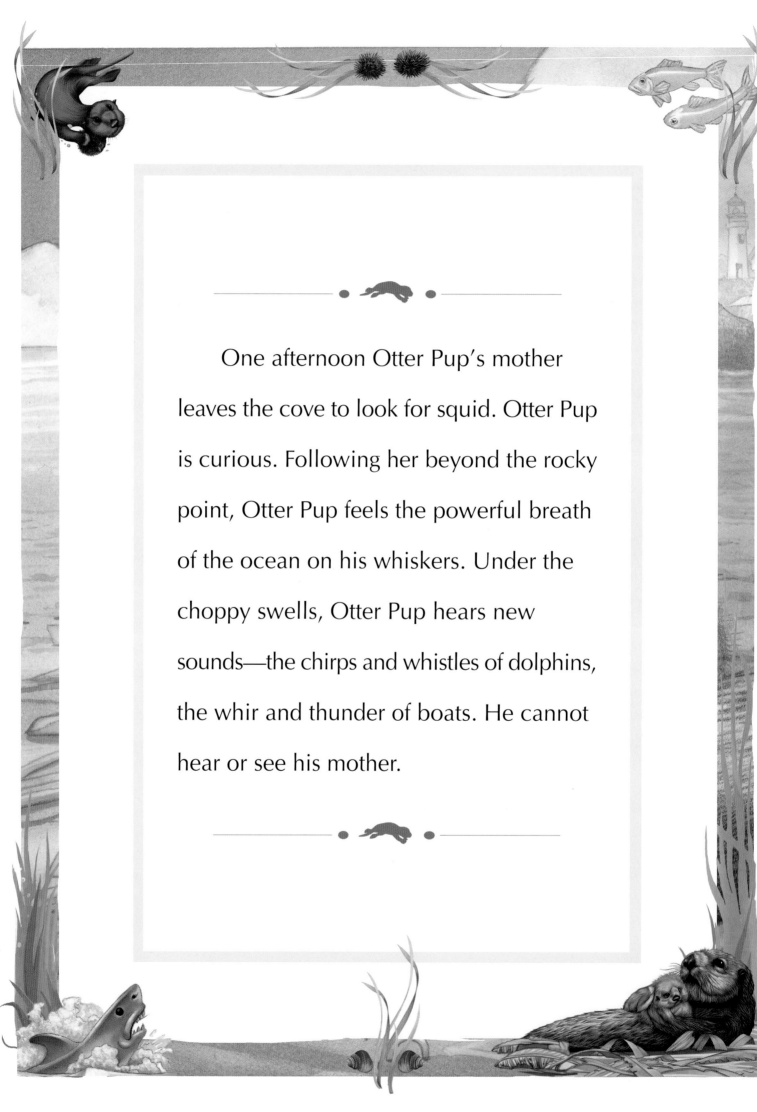

One afternoon Otter Pup's mother leaves the cove to look for squid. Otter Pup is curious. Following her beyond the rocky point, Otter Pup feels the powerful breath of the ocean on his whiskers. Under the choppy swells, Otter Pup hears new sounds—the chirps and whistles of dolphins, the whir and thunder of boats. He cannot hear or see his mother.

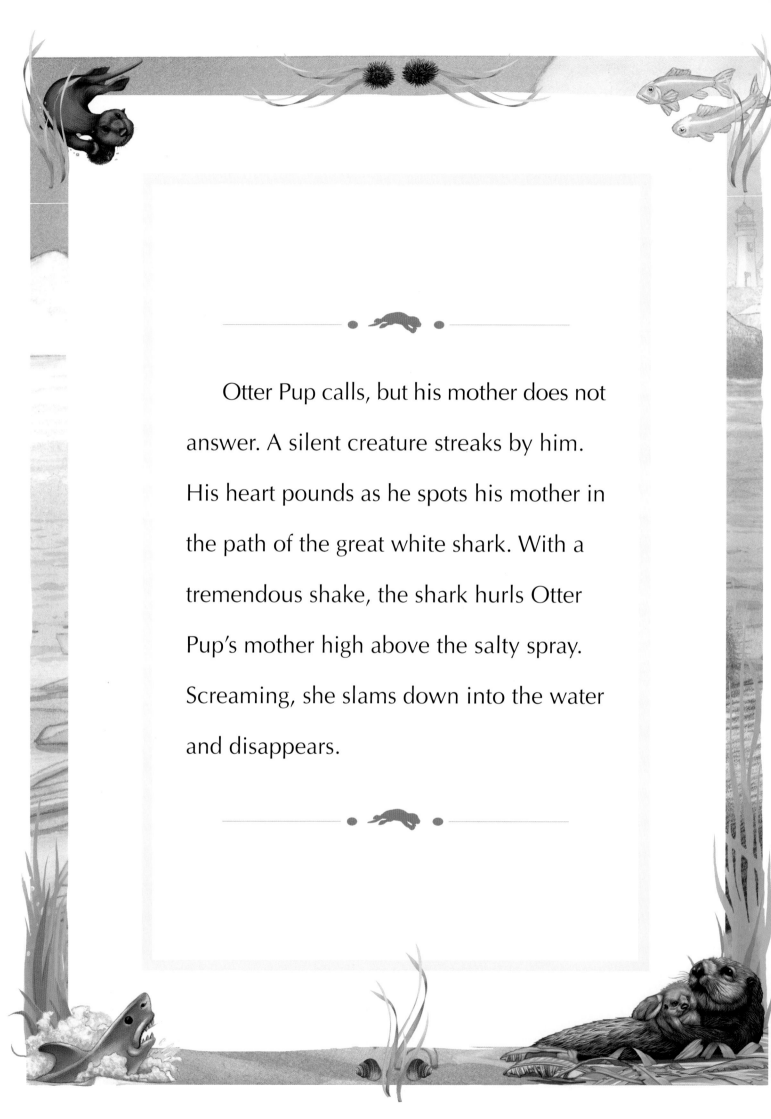

Otter Pup calls, but his mother does not answer. A silent creature streaks by him. His heart pounds as he spots his mother in the path of the great white shark. With a tremendous shake, the shark hurls Otter Pup's mother high above the salty spray. Screaming, she slams down into the water and disappears.

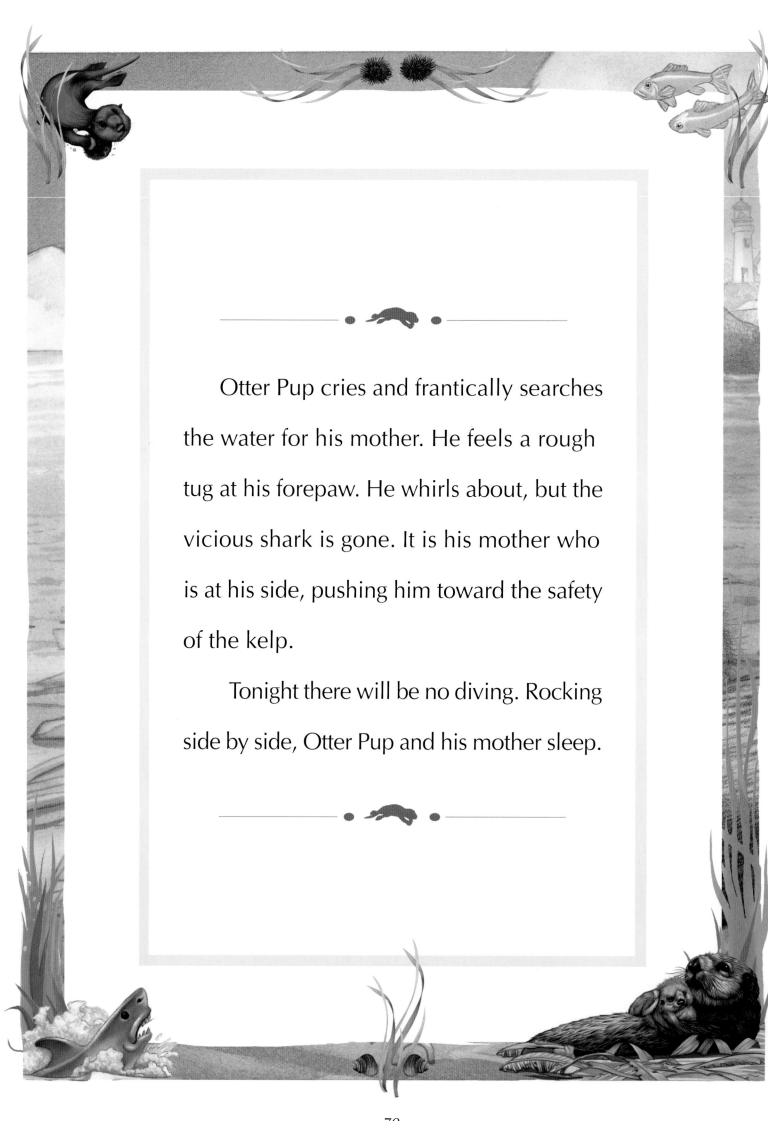

Otter Pup cries and frantically searches the water for his mother. He feels a rough tug at his forepaw. He whirls about, but the vicious shark is gone. It is his mother who is at his side, pushing him toward the safety of the kelp.

Tonight there will be no diving. Rocking side by side, Otter Pup and his mother sleep.

By summer's end, Otter Pup is almost fully grown. The world beyond the cove is full of danger, but he is filled with a new curiosity and restlessness.

One morning Otter Pup leaves his mother. He swims out past the rocky point, out past the foghorn.

Today is Otter's first day on his own.

Sea Turtle

by Lorraine A. Jay
Illustrated by Katie Lee

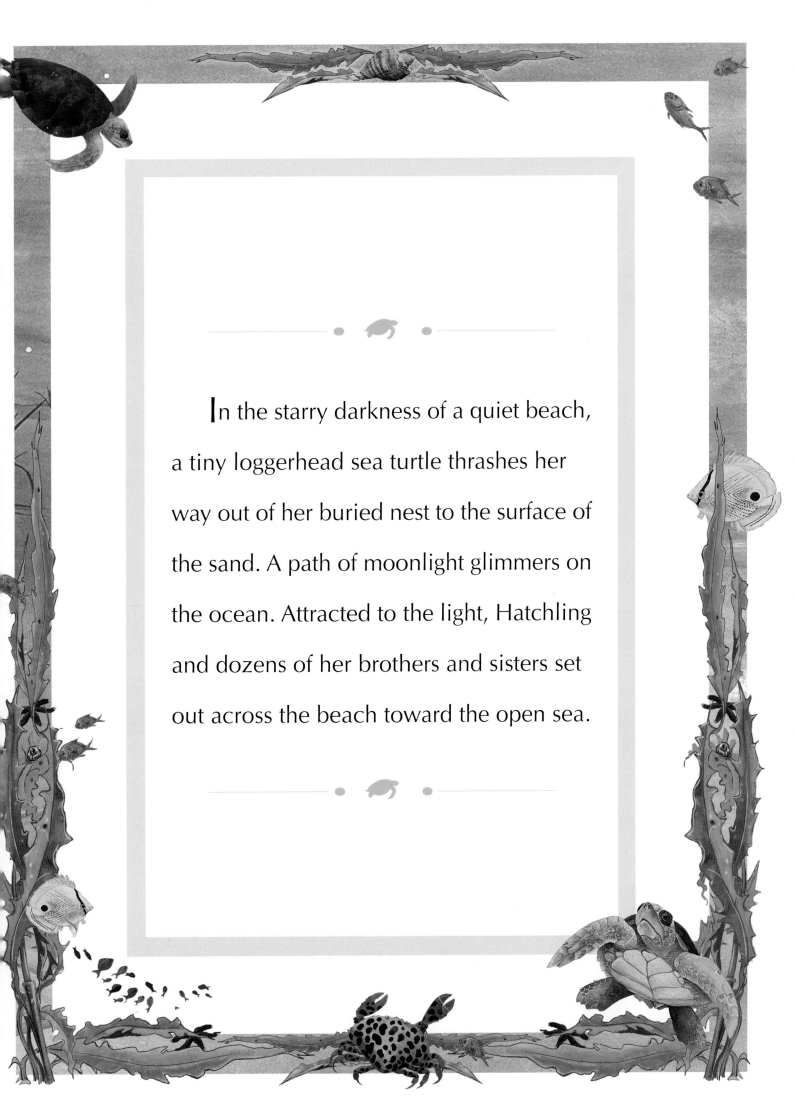

In the starry darkness of a quiet beach, a tiny loggerhead sea turtle thrashes her way out of her buried nest to the surface of the sand. A path of moonlight glimmers on the ocean. Attracted to the light, Hatchling and dozens of her brothers and sisters set out across the beach toward the open sea.

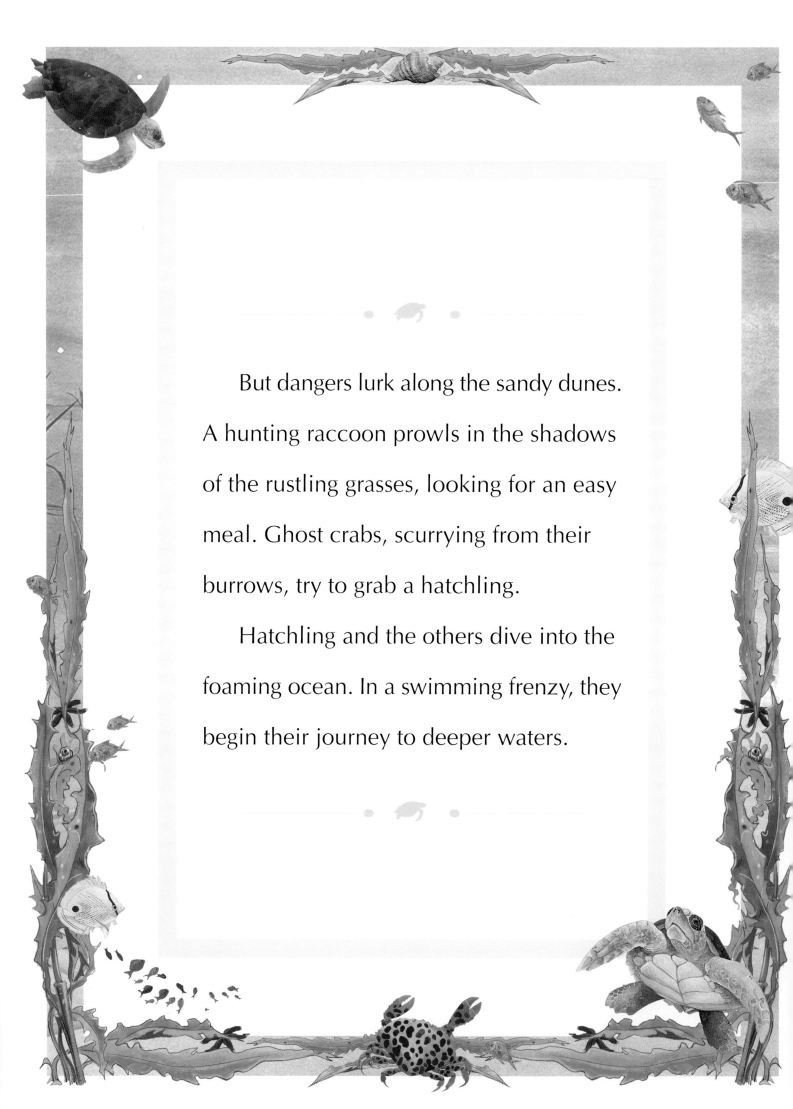

But dangers lurk along the sandy dunes. A hunting raccoon prowls in the shadows of the rustling grasses, looking for an easy meal. Ghost crabs, scurrying from their burrows, try to grab a hatchling.

Hatchling and the others dive into the foaming ocean. In a swimming frenzy, they begin their journey to deeper waters.

At first light, Hatchling is far from shore. All day and through the night, she swims on and on. Many miles out to sea, she climbs into a raft of seaweed and sleeps.

In the morning, Hatchling discovers that the seaweed is full of tasty foods—little fishes, crabs and jellyfish. Chomping on a shrimp, Loggerhead Hatchling eats her first meal.

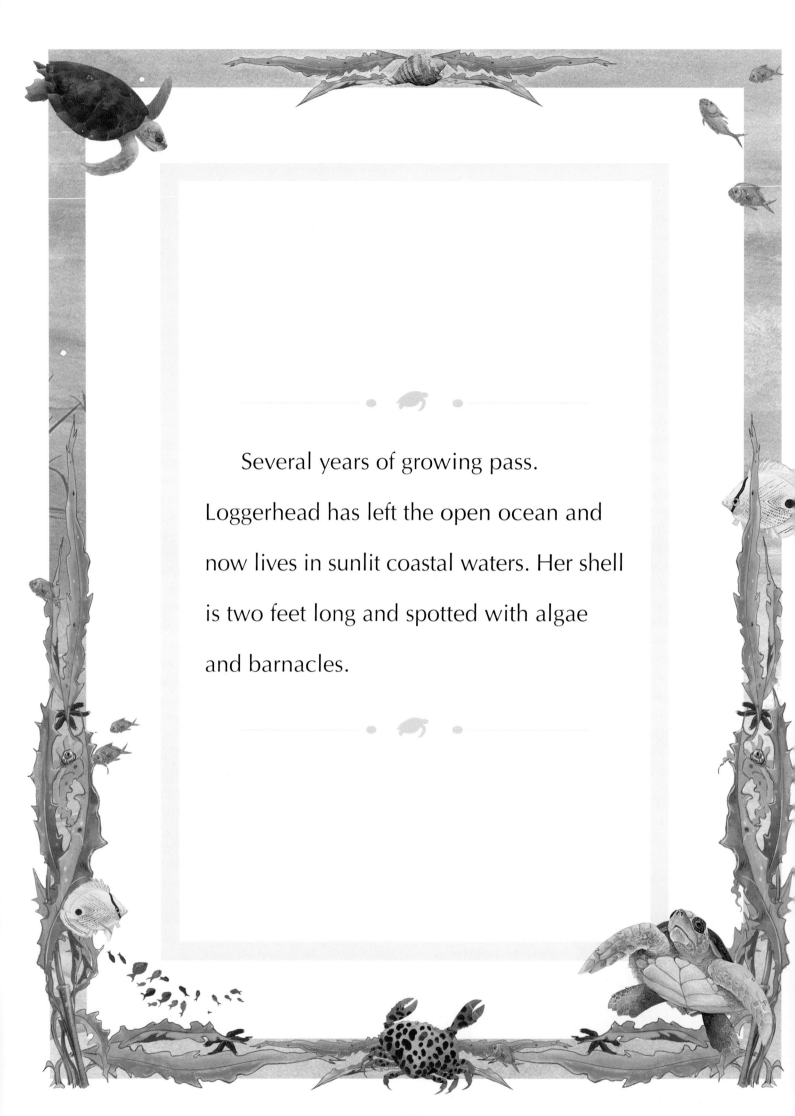

Several years of growing pass.
Loggerhead has left the open ocean and
now lives in sunlit coastal waters. Her shell
is two feet long and spotted with algae
and barnacles.

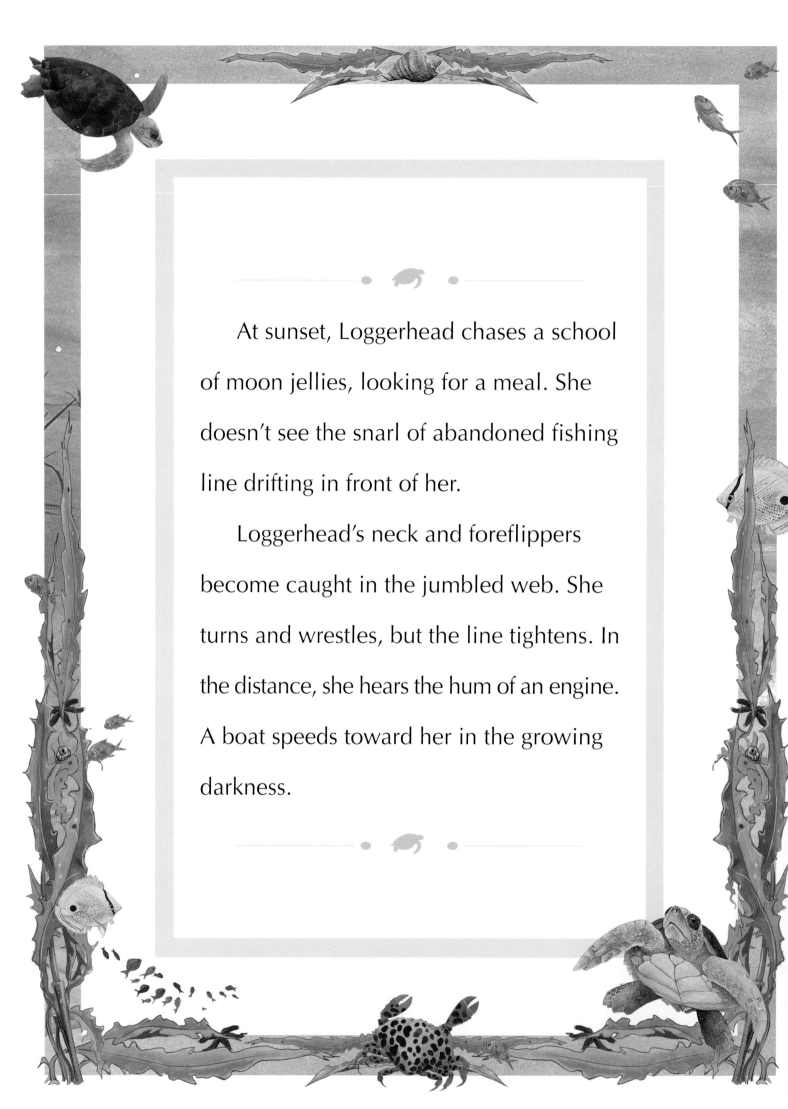

At sunset, Loggerhead chases a school of moon jellies, looking for a meal. She doesn't see the snarl of abandoned fishing line drifting in front of her.

Loggerhead's neck and foreflippers become caught in the jumbled web. She turns and wrestles, but the line tightens. In the distance, she hears the hum of an engine. A boat speeds toward her in the growing darkness.

Loggerhead is trapped! With all her strength, she forces her mighty foreflippers down.

Snap! The line breaks. Again she strains every muscle, moving her flippers up and down to loosen the line around her. At last, she is free. She dives, just missing the propeller as the boat zooms past.

Year after year, Loggerhead travels through hundreds of miles of ocean. As she grows, she explores coral reefs and warm lagoons. Even at three hundred pounds, she swims with grace and ease.

Late one spring, she begins the journey back to the beach where she was born. Mysteriously, she knows how to find her way.

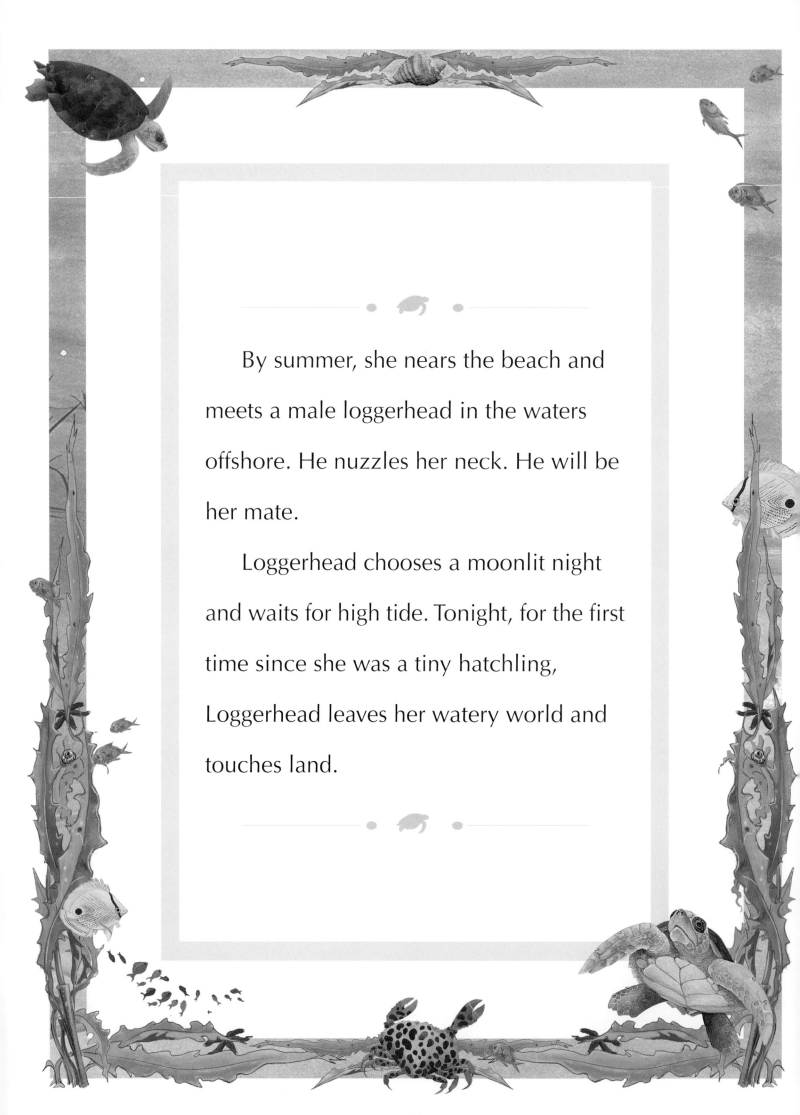

By summer, she nears the beach and meets a male loggerhead in the waters offshore. He nuzzles her neck. He will be her mate.

Loggerhead chooses a moonlit night and waits for high tide. Tonight, for the first time since she was a tiny hatchling, Loggerhead leaves her watery world and touches land.

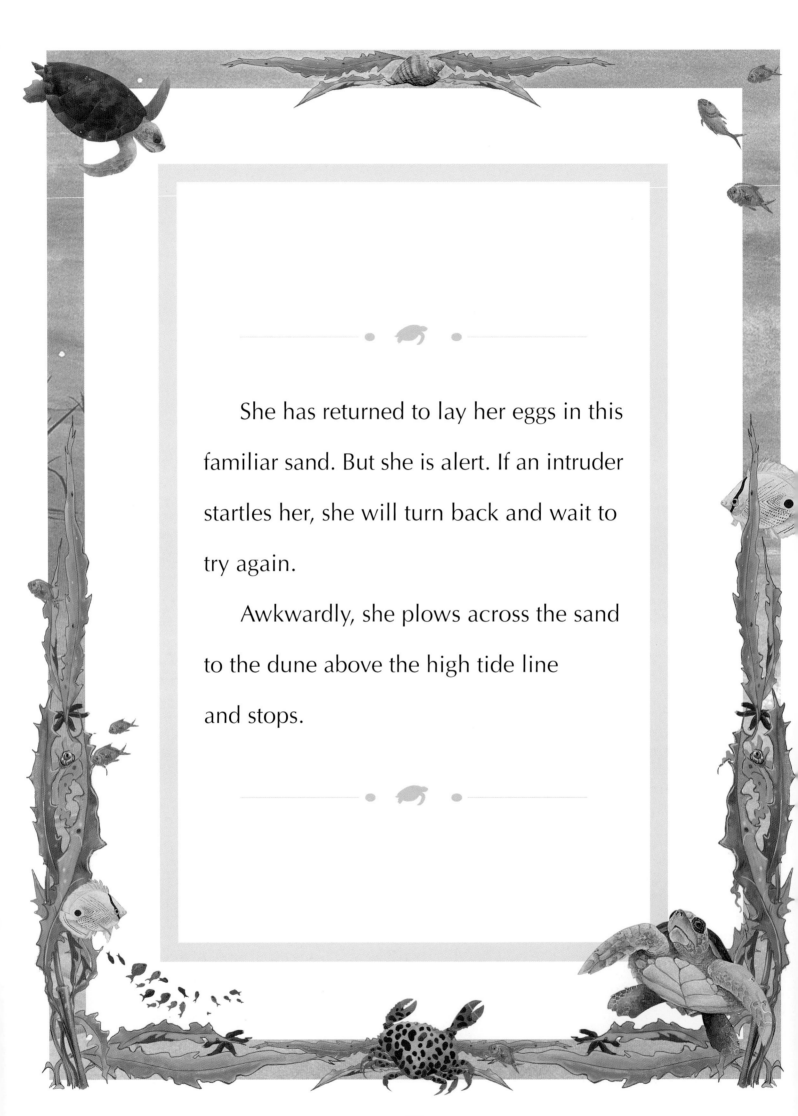

She has returned to lay her eggs in this familiar sand. But she is alert. If an intruder startles her, she will turn back and wait to try again.

Awkwardly, she plows across the sand to the dune above the high tide line and stops.

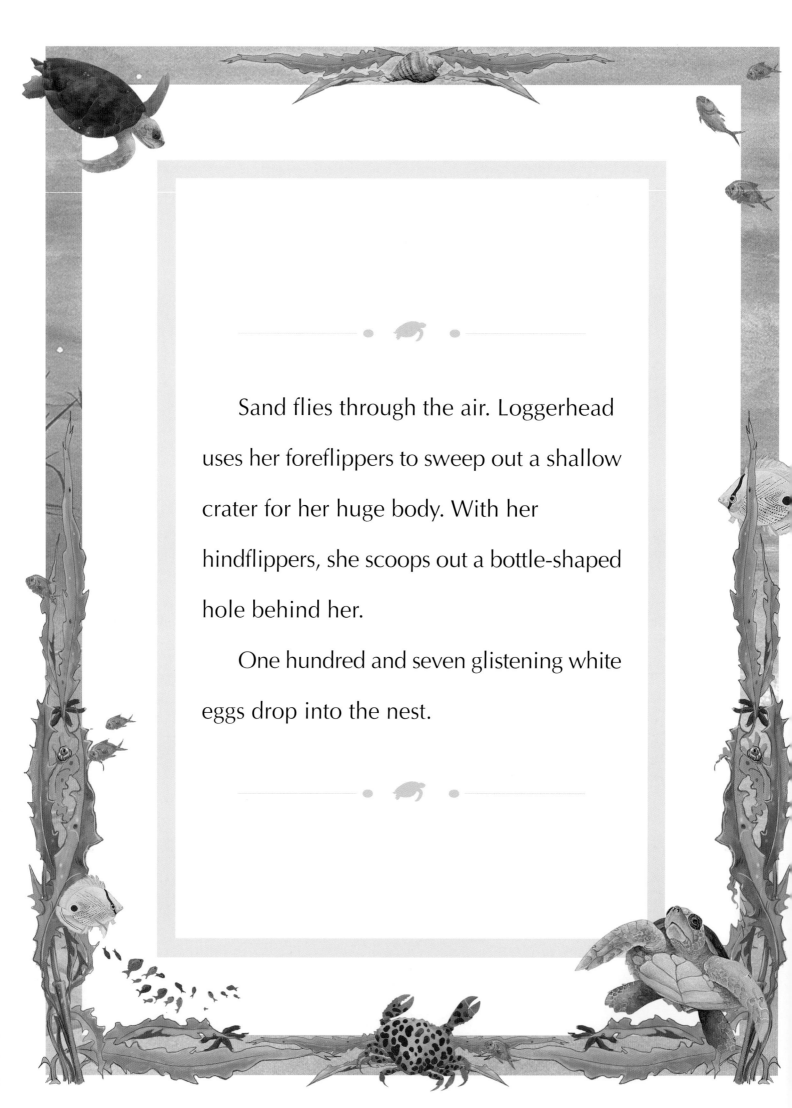

Sand flies through the air. Loggerhead uses her foreflippers to sweep out a shallow crater for her huge body. With her hindflippers, she scoops out a bottle-shaped hole behind her.

One hundred and seven glistening white eggs drop into the nest.

Loggerhead pats sand over her precious eggs, hiding them from predators. Now, following a moonlit path, she tracks back to the sea and disappears into the water.

Two months later, under a starry sky, a loggerhead hatchling emerges from the sand. With all her brothers and all her sisters, she scuttles across the beach and begins her journey to the open sea.

Walrus

by Carol Young
Illustrated by Walter Stuart

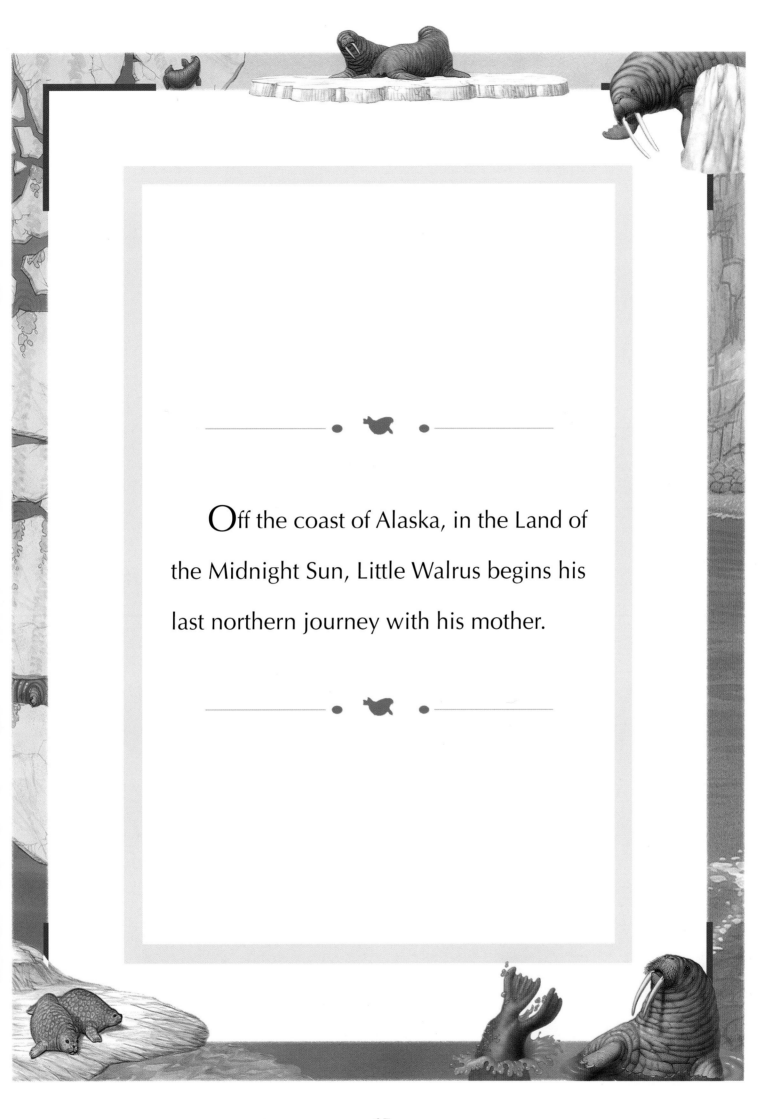

Off the coast of Alaska, in the Land of the Midnight Sun, Little Walrus begins his last northern journey with his mother.

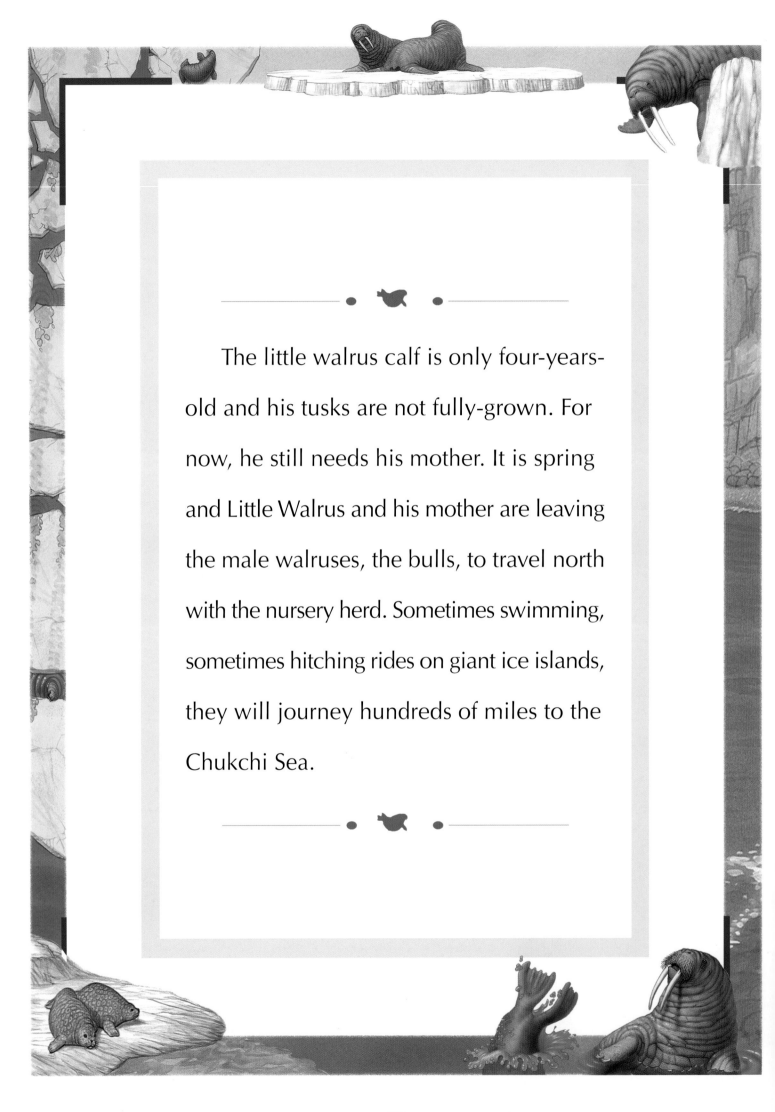

The little walrus calf is only four-years-old and his tusks are not fully-grown. For now, he still needs his mother. It is spring and Little Walrus and his mother are leaving the male walruses, the bulls, to travel north with the nursery herd. Sometimes swimming, sometimes hitching rides on giant ice islands, they will journey hundreds of miles to the Chukchi Sea.

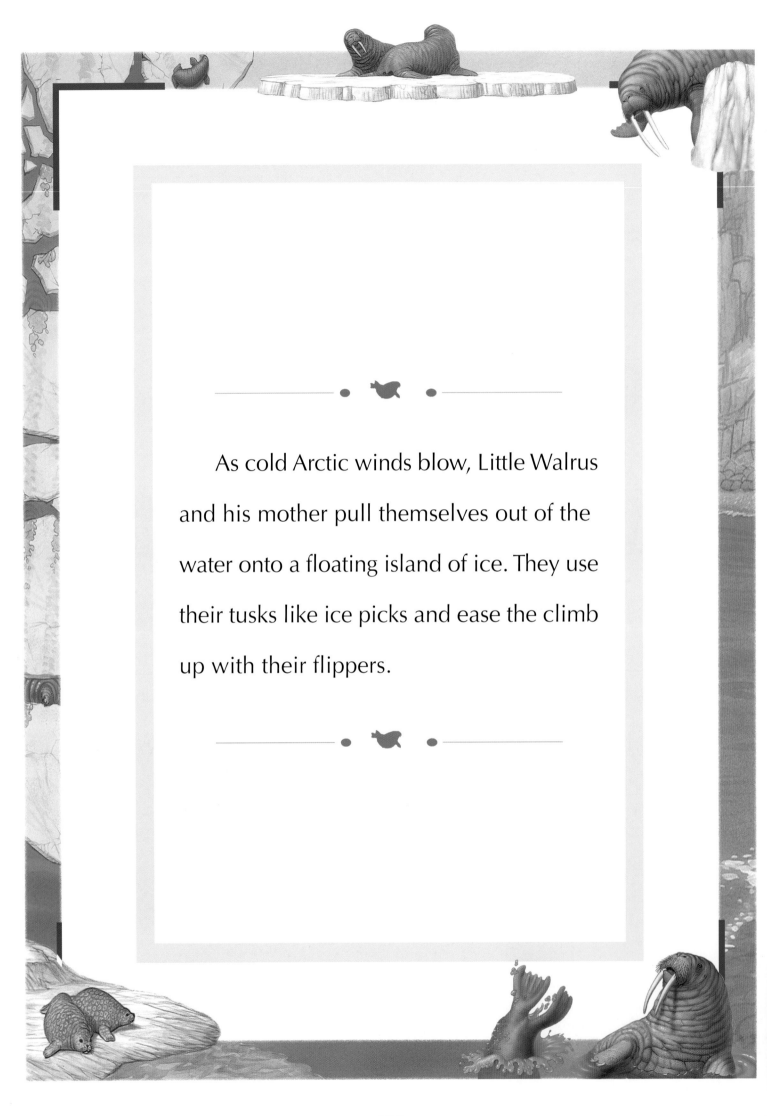

As cold Arctic winds blow, Little Walrus
and his mother pull themselves out of the
water onto a floating island of ice. They use
their tusks like ice picks and ease the climb
up with their flippers.

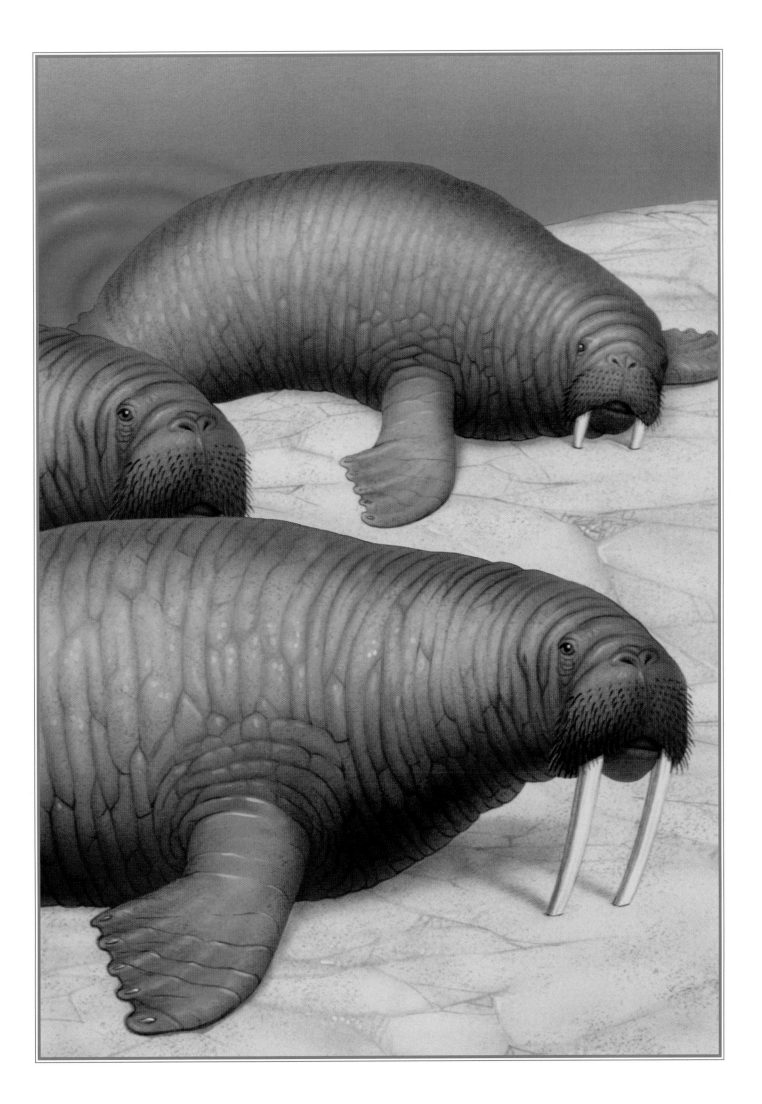

As Mother moves across the ice, Little
Walrus lags further and further behind.
Slipping and sliding, he falls between giant
wedges of ice.

Hearing his pitiful cry, Mother hurries
to Little Walrus. Chips fly as she frantically
hacks at the ice. Steadily, she opens a way
of escape and helps Little Walrus to safety.

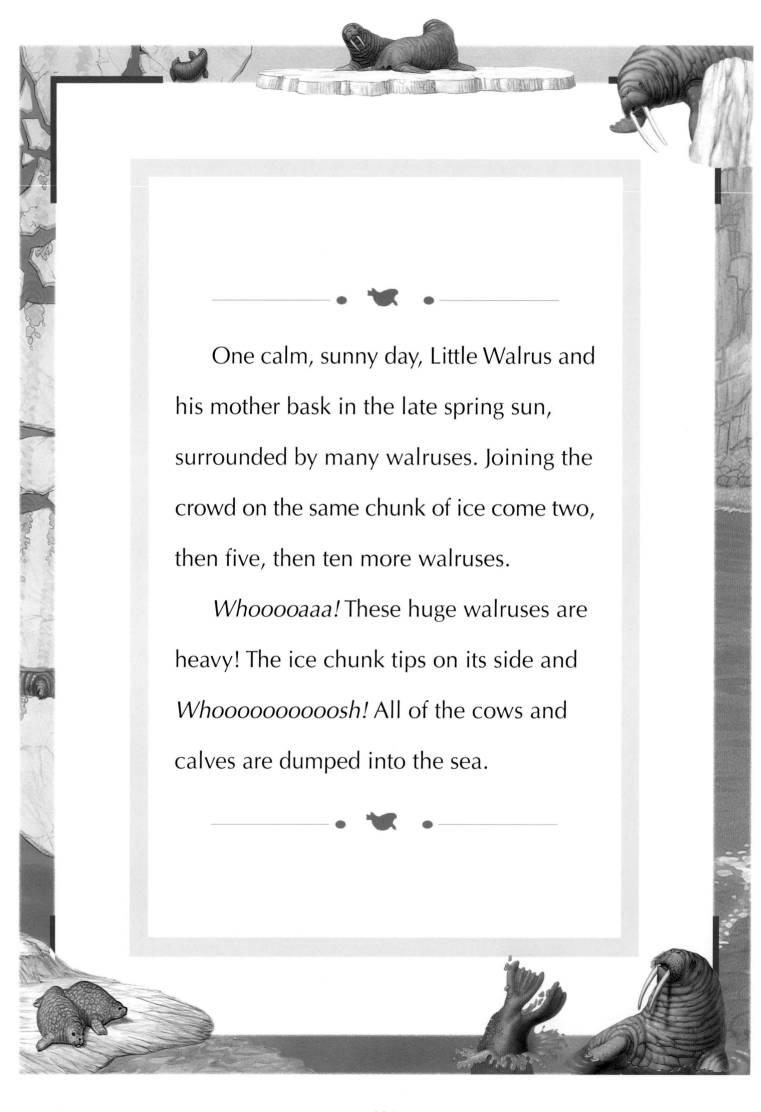

One calm, sunny day, Little Walrus and
his mother bask in the late spring sun,
surrounded by many walruses. Joining the
crowd on the same chunk of ice come two,
then five, then ten more walruses.

Whooooaaa! These huge walruses are
heavy! The ice chunk tips on its side and
Whooooooooooosh! All of the cows and
calves are dumped into the sea.

Splash! Crash!

There is so much confusion! Little Walrus' mother swims in search of her calf. When she finally finds him, he is not in the water at all! He was the first walrus in the nursery herd to pull himself onto another chunk of ice.

As summer arrives, the herd reaches the Chukchi Sea. Now it is time for Little Walrus to learn to hunt on his own.

One summer day, Little Walrus waits on the edge of the ice. He does not want to dive into the ice-cold water alone. His mother comes up from behind and pushes him into the Chukchi Sea.

Kerplunk!

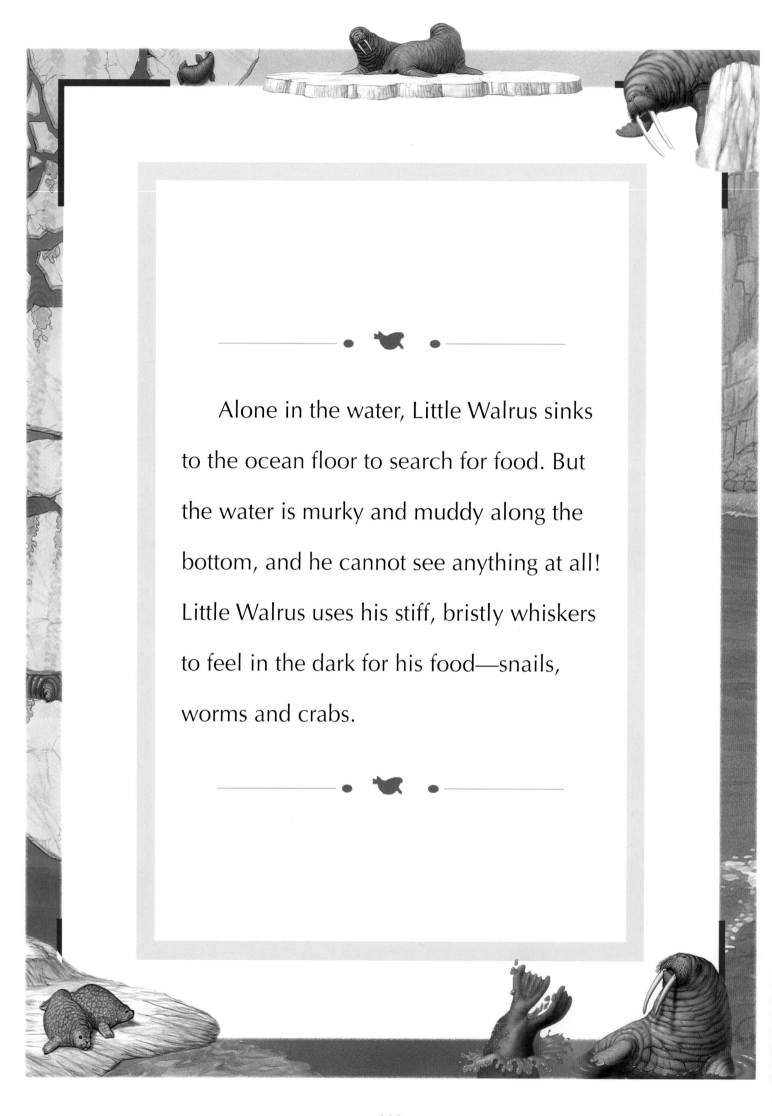

Alone in the water, Little Walrus sinks to the ocean floor to search for food. But the water is murky and muddy along the bottom, and he cannot see anything at all! Little Walrus uses his stiff, bristly whiskers to feel in the dark for his food—snails, worms and crabs.

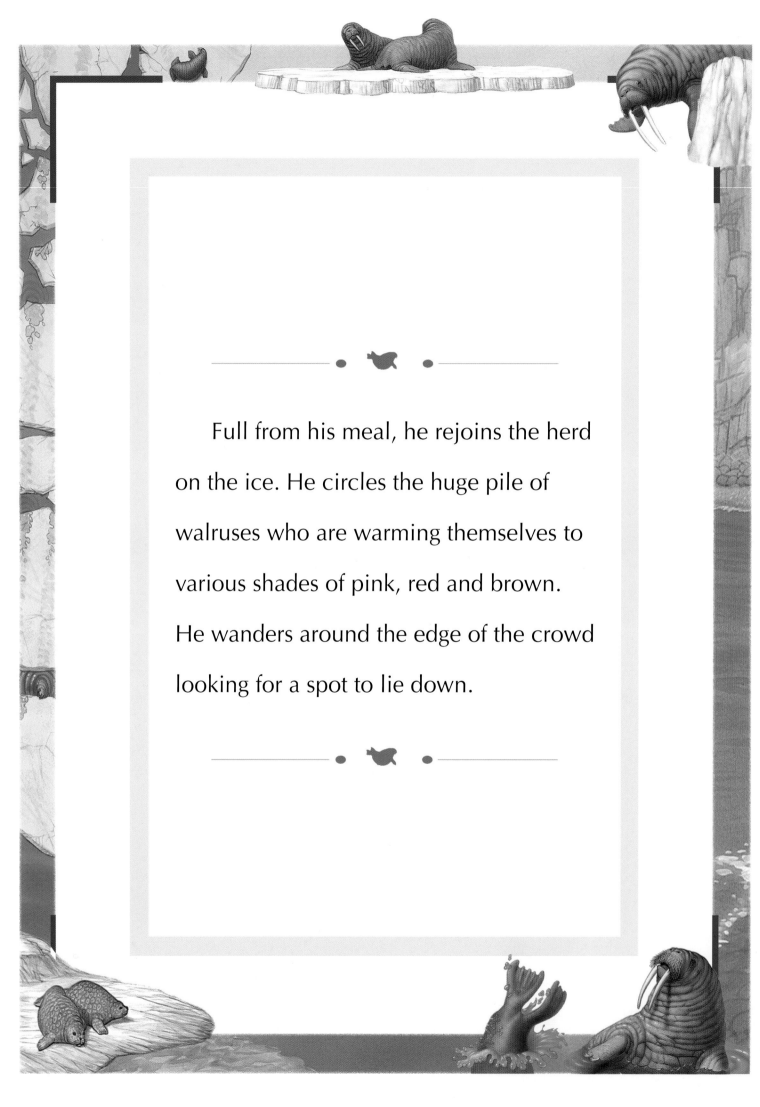

Full from his meal, he rejoins the herd
on the ice. He circles the huge pile of
walruses who are warming themselves to
various shades of pink, red and brown.
He wanders around the edge of the crowd
looking for a spot to lie down.

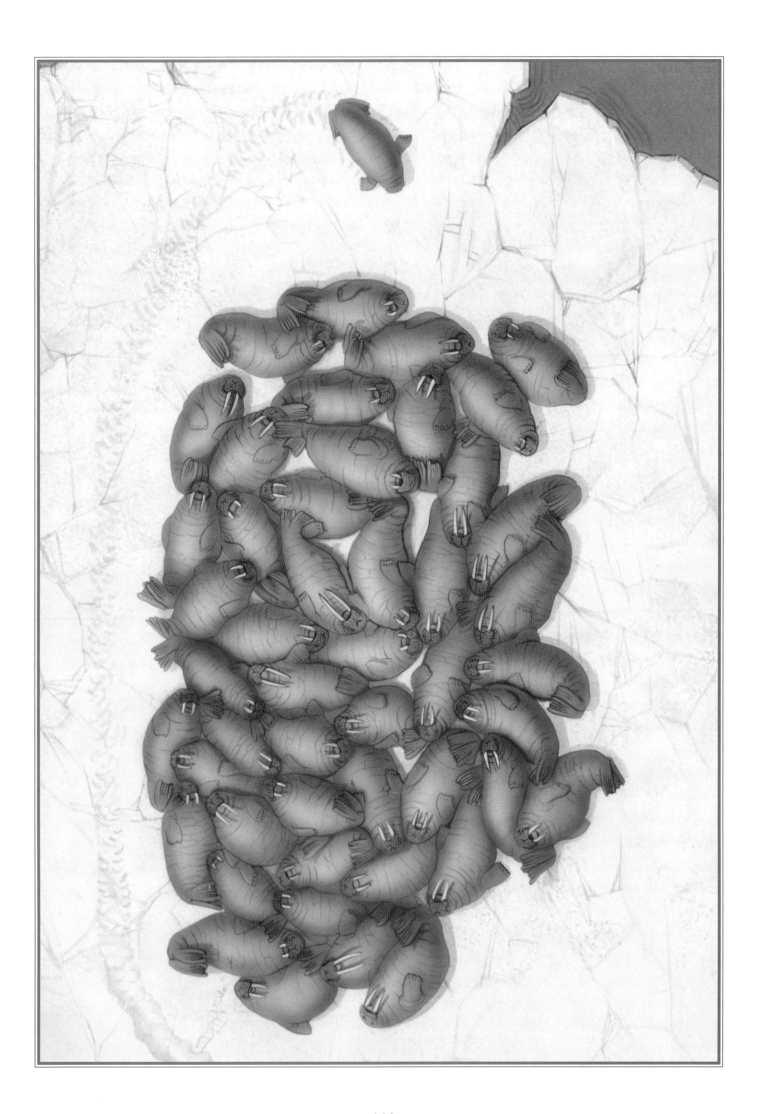

113

Suddenly sniffing the wind, Little Walrus smells danger. He cannot see the threat, for the enemy is the color of ice and snow. Little Walrus lifts his head and thrusts his tusks high in the sky. Little Walrus lets out a ROAR—a warning for all to hear!

The older walruses grunt and growl. The younger ones bark and cry. Their monstrous sounds and the sight of so many gleaming white tusks frighten the creature away. The polar bear retreats into the landscape of snow and ice to search for an easier meal.

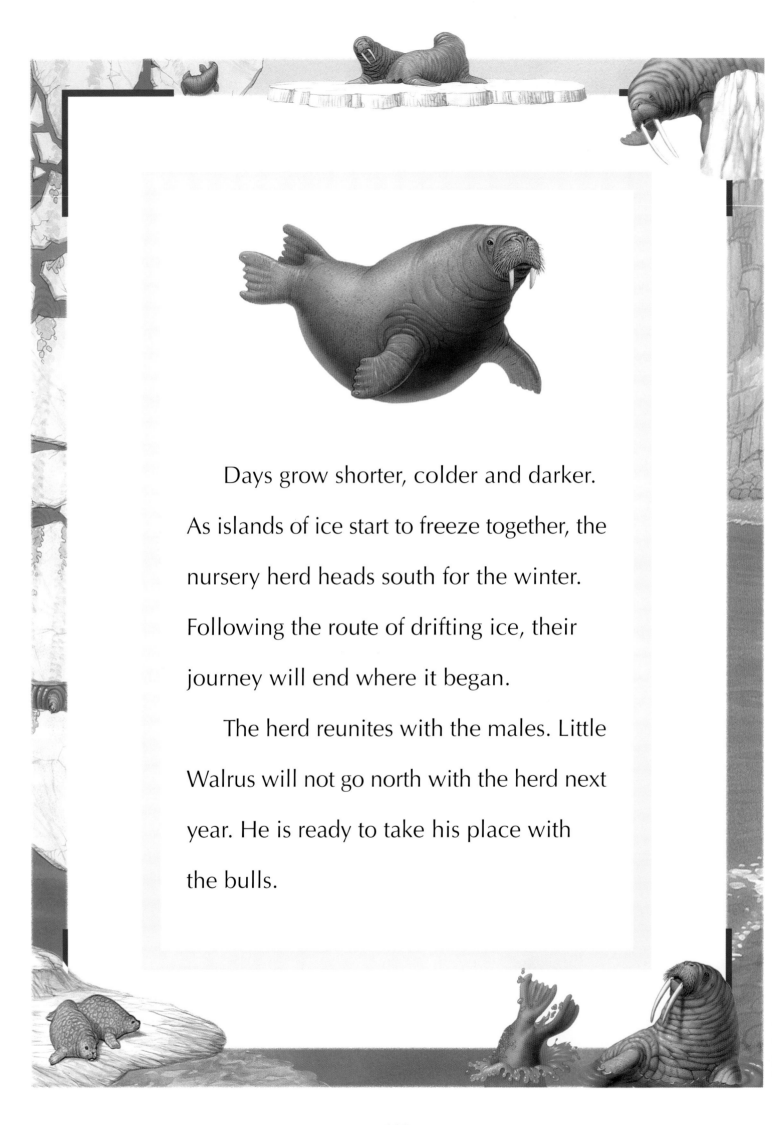

Days grow shorter, colder and darker. As islands of ice start to freeze together, the nursery herd heads south for the winter. Following the route of drifting ice, their journey will end where it began.

The herd reunites with the males. Little Walrus will not go north with the herd next year. He is ready to take his place with the bulls.

Humpback Whale

by Darice Bailer
Illustrated by Stephen Marchesi

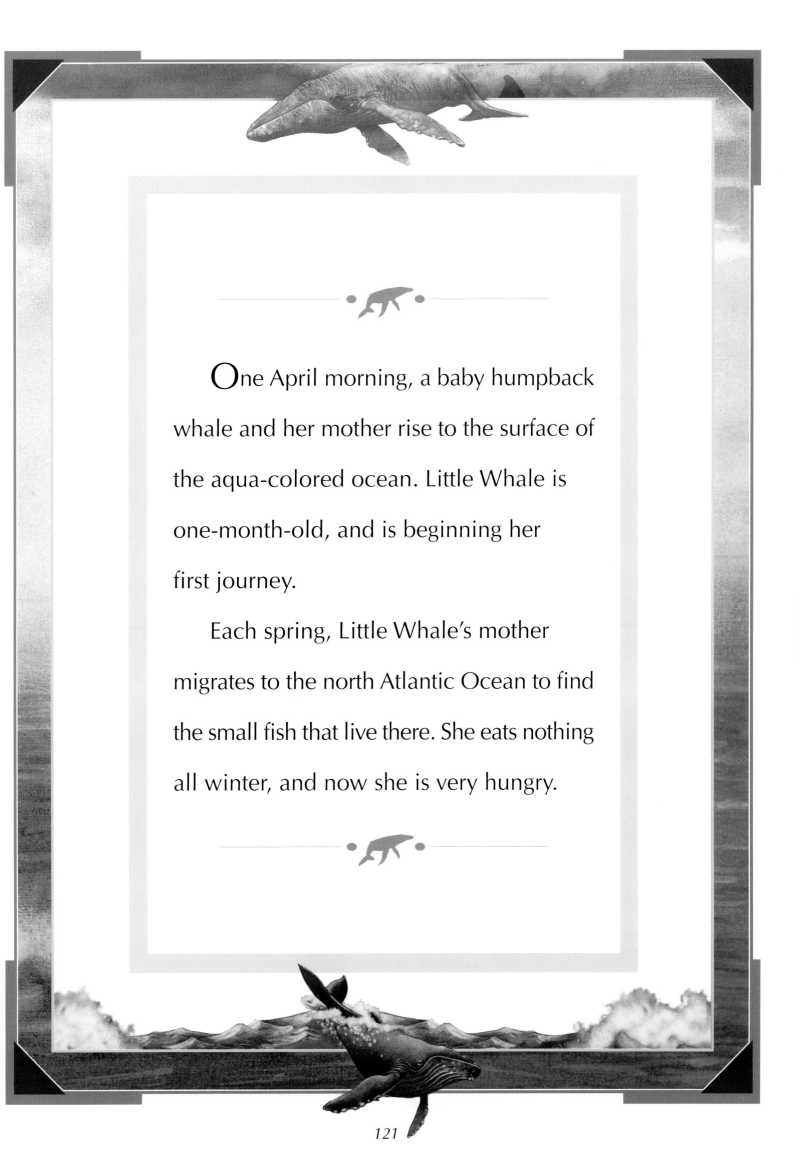

One April morning, a baby humpback whale and her mother rise to the surface of the aqua-colored ocean. Little Whale is one-month-old, and is beginning her first journey.

Each spring, Little Whale's mother migrates to the north Atlantic Ocean to find the small fish that live there. She eats nothing all winter, and now she is very hungry.

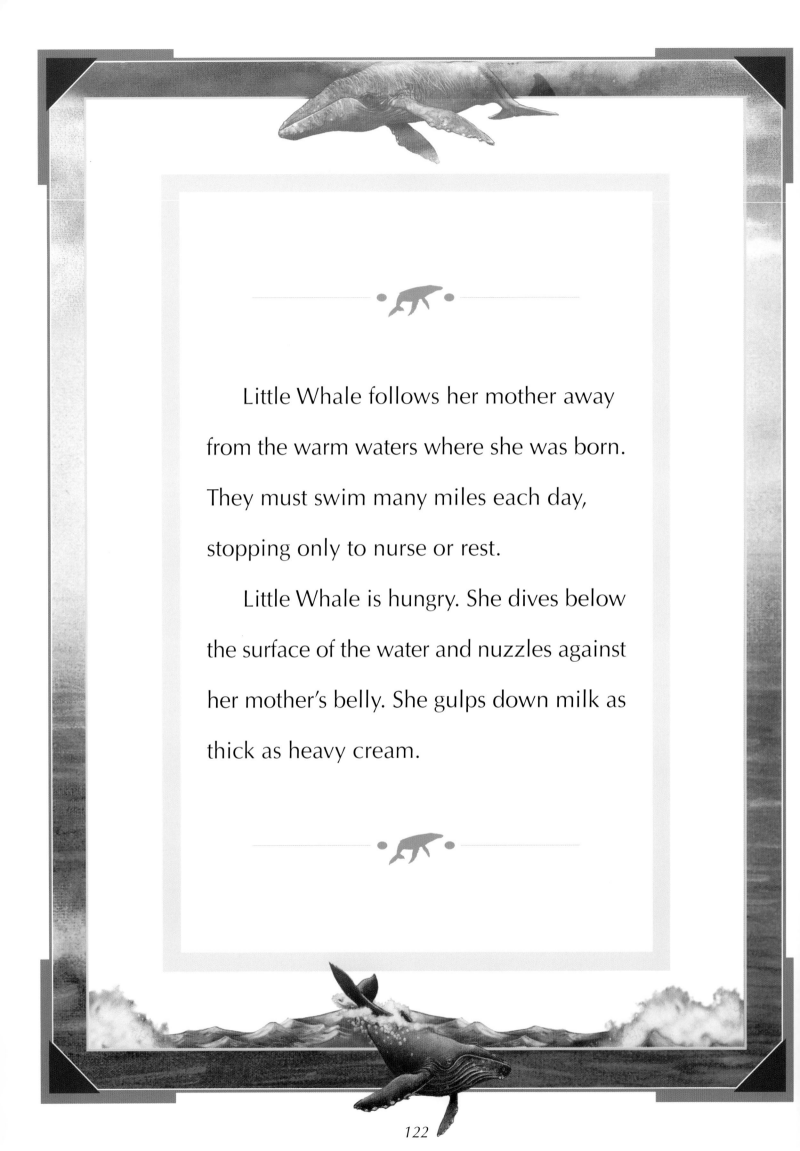

Little Whale follows her mother away from the warm waters where she was born. They must swim many miles each day, stopping only to nurse or rest.

Little Whale is hungry. She dives below the surface of the water and nuzzles against her mother's belly. She gulps down milk as thick as heavy cream.

Little Whale must soon come to the surface to breathe. Little Whale's lungs are still small and she can only stay under water for minutes at a time. She exhales through the two blowholes on top of her head. Her mother surfaces alongside her and blasts a misty plume of spray high into the air!

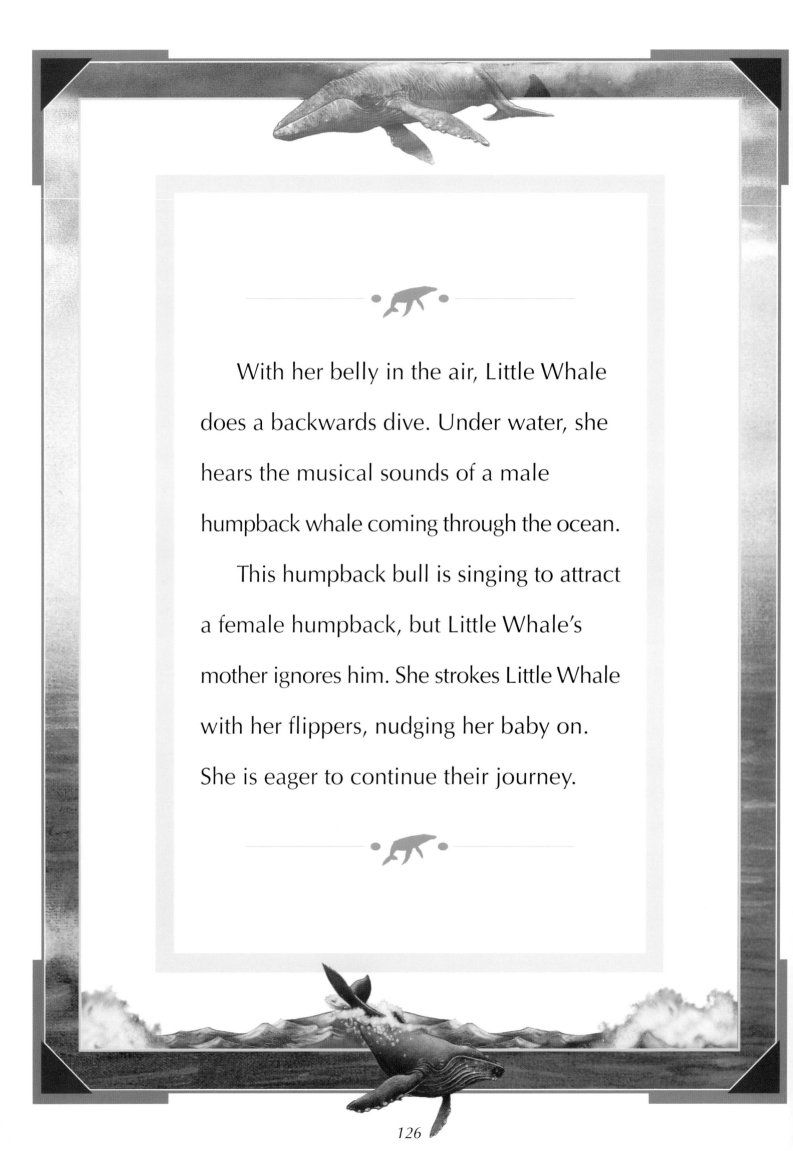

With her belly in the air, Little Whale does a backwards dive. Under water, she hears the musical sounds of a male humpback whale coming through the ocean.

This humpback bull is singing to attract a female humpback, but Little Whale's mother ignores him. She strokes Little Whale with her flippers, nudging her baby on. She is eager to continue their journey.

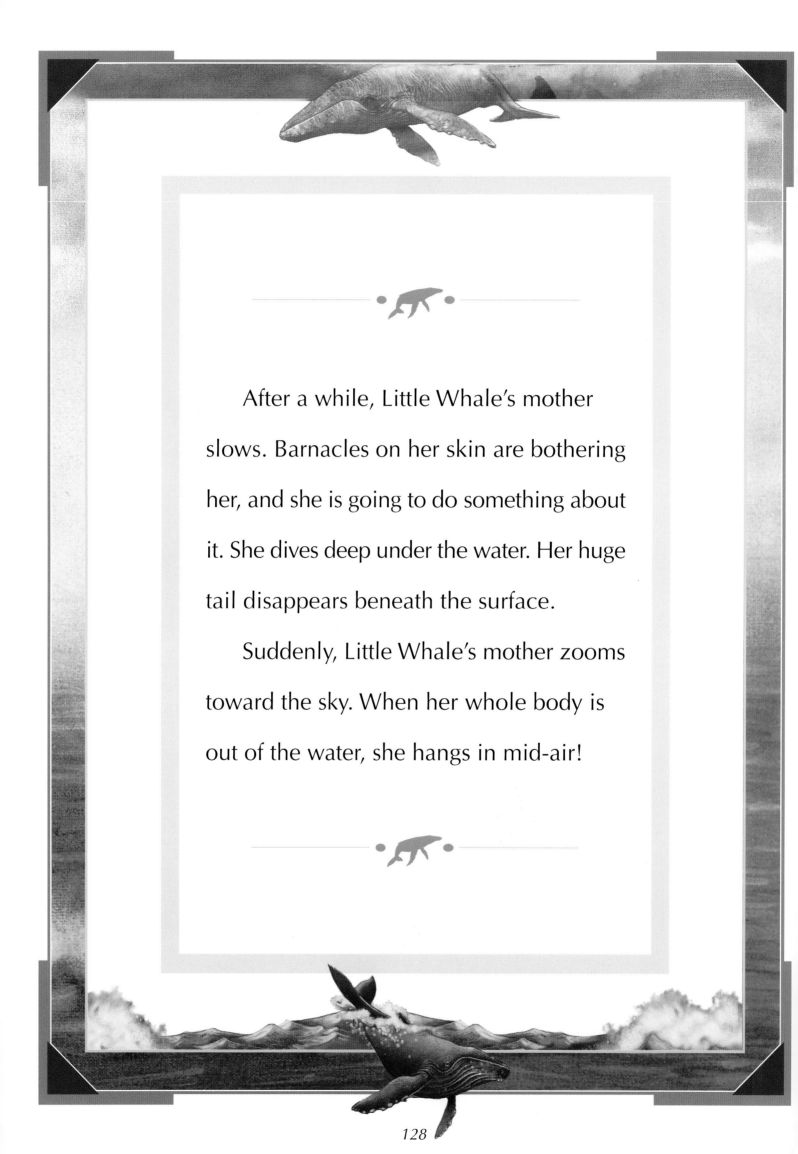

After a while, Little Whale's mother slows. Barnacles on her skin are bothering her, and she is going to do something about it. She dives deep under the water. Her huge tail disappears beneath the surface.

Suddenly, Little Whale's mother zooms toward the sky. When her whole body is out of the water, she hangs in mid-air!

Splash! She crashes down on her back on the surface of the ocean. That will knock off some of the bothersome barnacles! Fountains of water spray up around her, making waves that bounce Little Whale around.

Little Whale wants to copy her mother. She dives, but she cannot jump as high yet.

That night, Little Whale and her mother stop to rest in the calm water. Suddenly, Little Whale hears and feels the sea vibrating. The sharp-edged bow of a coast-guard cutter races toward her!

In the dark, the cutter's pilot cannot see Little Whale and her mother in the water. Little Whale's mother swoops in front of her baby to protect her. But, the cutter just misses them. It roars out of sight and the choppy waves subside. The danger has passed.

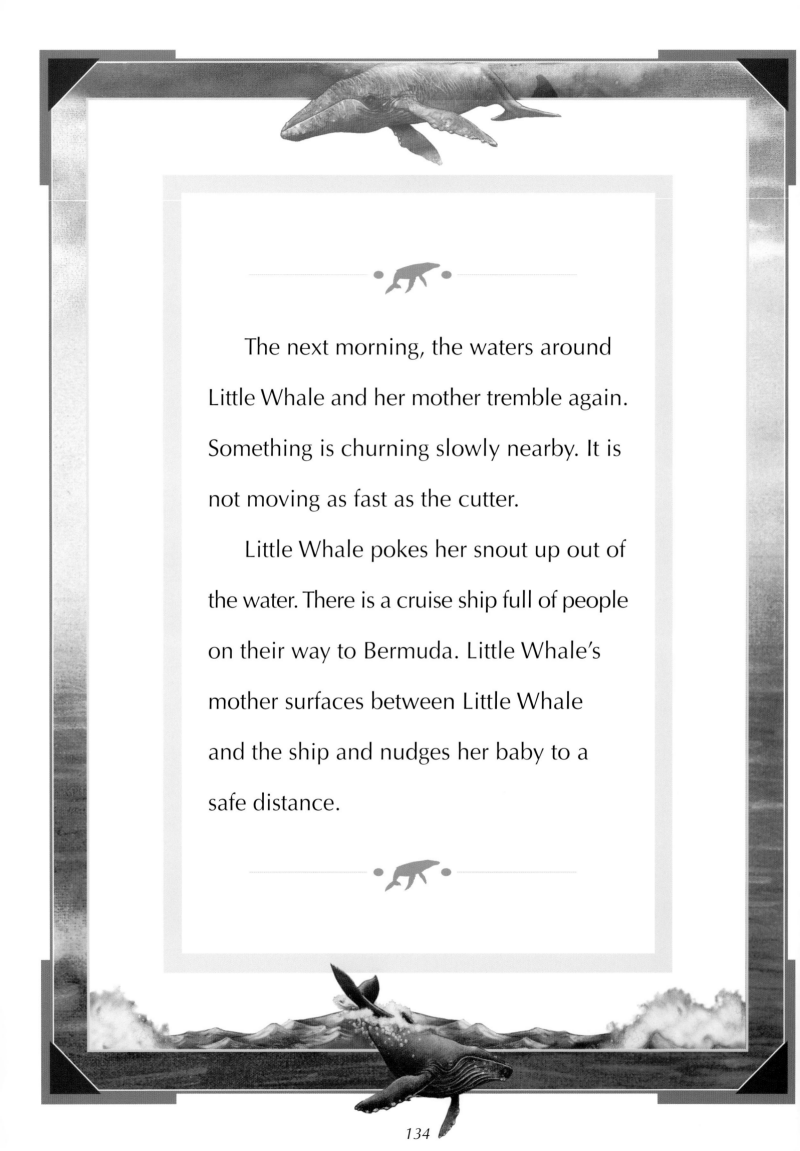

The next morning, the waters around Little Whale and her mother tremble again. Something is churning slowly nearby. It is not moving as fast as the cutter.

Little Whale pokes her snout up out of the water. There is a cruise ship full of people on their way to Bermuda. Little Whale's mother surfaces between Little Whale and the ship and nudges her baby to a safe distance.

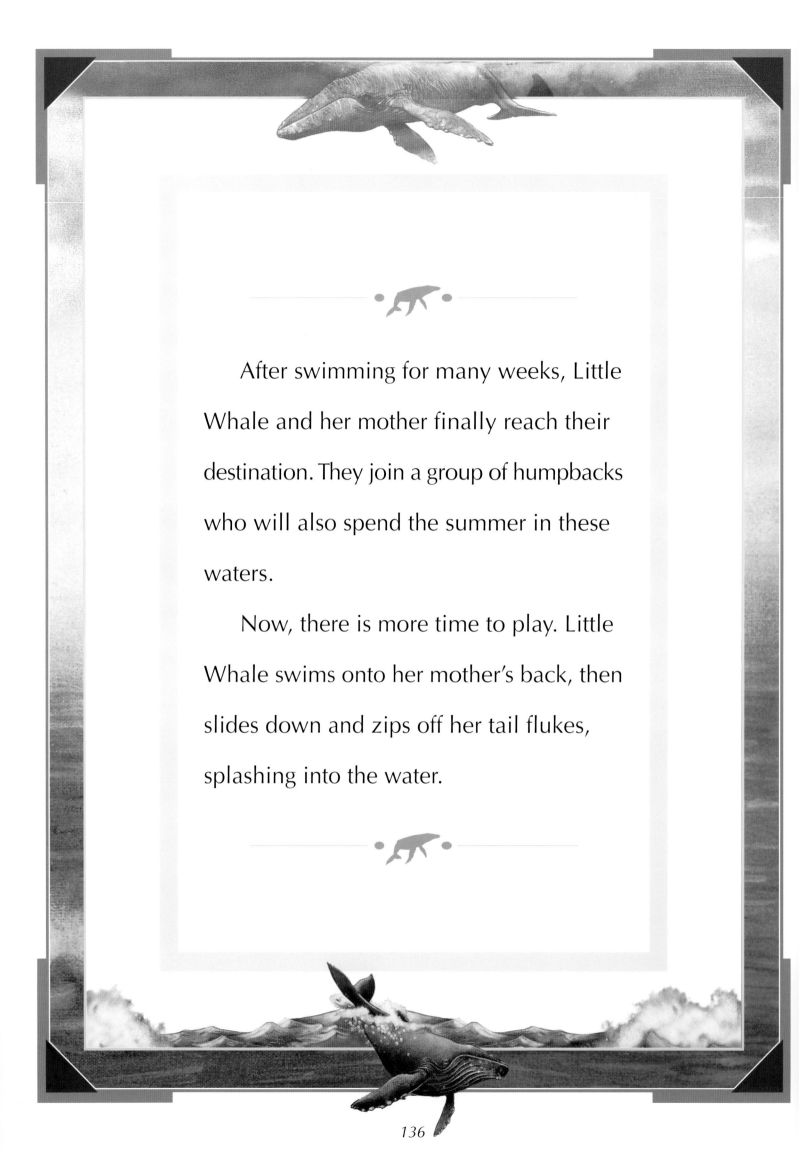

After swimming for many weeks, Little
Whale and her mother finally reach their
destination. They join a group of humpbacks
who will also spend the summer in these
waters.

Now, there is more time to play. Little
Whale swims onto her mother's back, then
slides down and zips off her tail flukes,
splashing into the water.

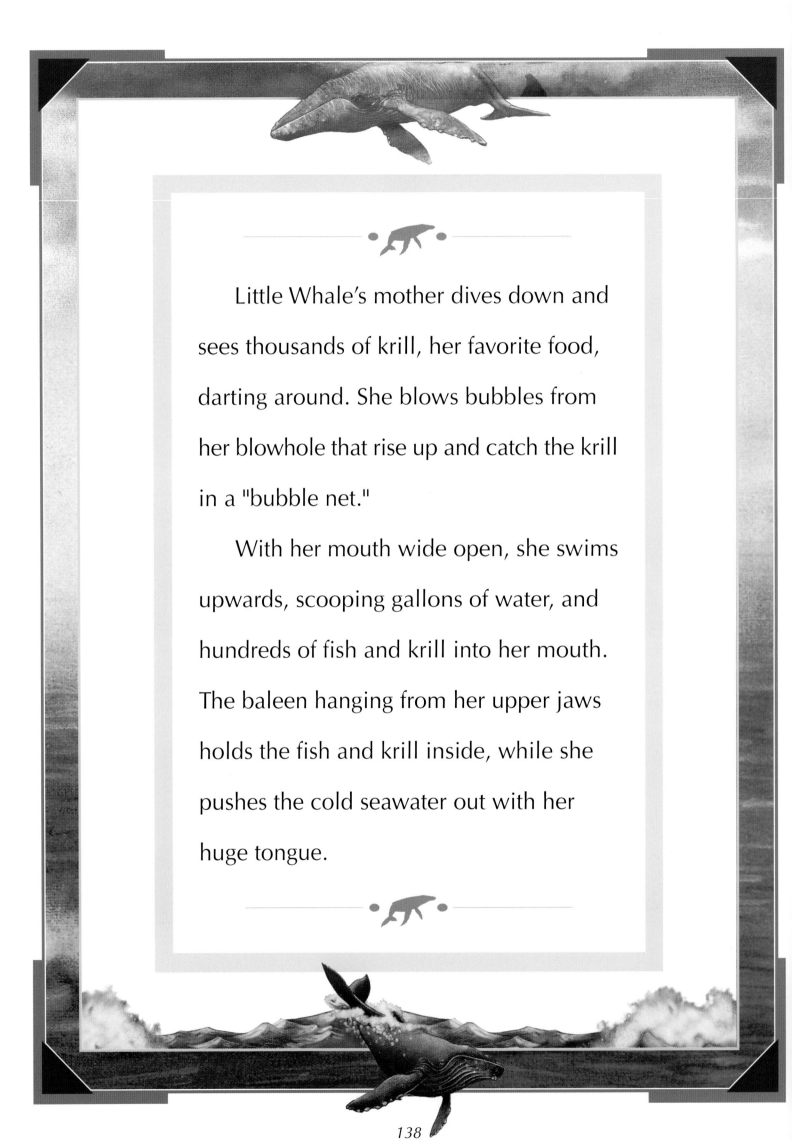

Little Whale's mother dives down and sees thousands of krill, her favorite food, darting around. She blows bubbles from her blowhole that rise up and catch the krill in a "bubble net."

With her mouth wide open, she swims upwards, scooping gallons of water, and hundreds of fish and krill into her mouth. The baleen hanging from her upper jaws holds the fish and krill inside, while she pushes the cold seawater out with her huge tongue.

After Little Whale's mother fills her belly, she begins to play, too. She slaps the water with her tail. Water splashes all around!

The day is coming to an end. The sky is royal blue and the lowering sun is gold, but Little Whale doesn't want to rest yet. She is too busy playing in the deep green ocean, safely at her mother's side.

Octopus

by Deirdre Langeland
Illustrated by Steven James Petruccio

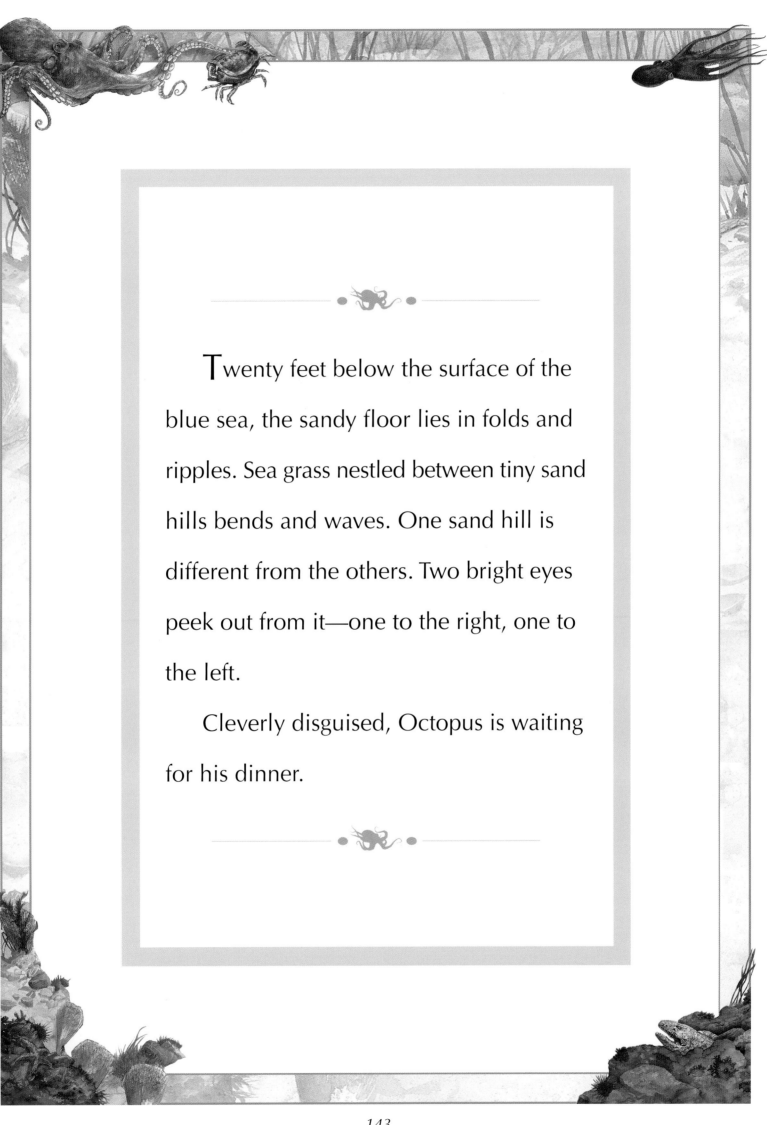

Twenty feet below the surface of the blue sea, the sandy floor lies in folds and ripples. Sea grass nestled between tiny sand hills bends and waves. One sand hill is different from the others. Two bright eyes peek out from it—one to the right, one to the left.

Cleverly disguised, Octopus is waiting for his dinner.

Before long, a crab creeps by. It scuttles sideways on hard-shelled legs. Close, close, closer. Suddenly one of Octopus' long arms shoots out and the crab is caught. It cannot break free from Octopus' strong suction cups.

Octopus uses his sharp beak to break open the crab's shell and eat his tasty meal.

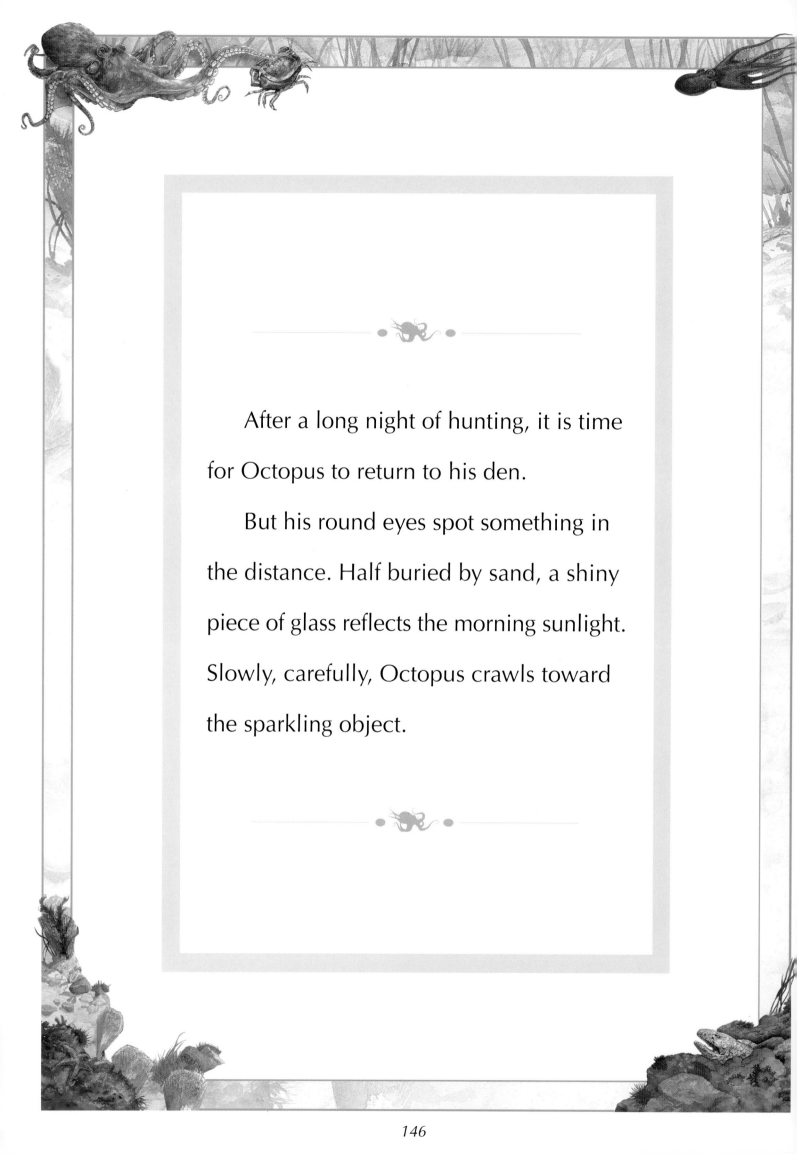

After a long night of hunting, it is time for Octopus to return to his den.

But his round eyes spot something in the distance. Half buried by sand, a shiny piece of glass reflects the morning sunlight. Slowly, carefully, Octopus crawls toward the sparkling object.

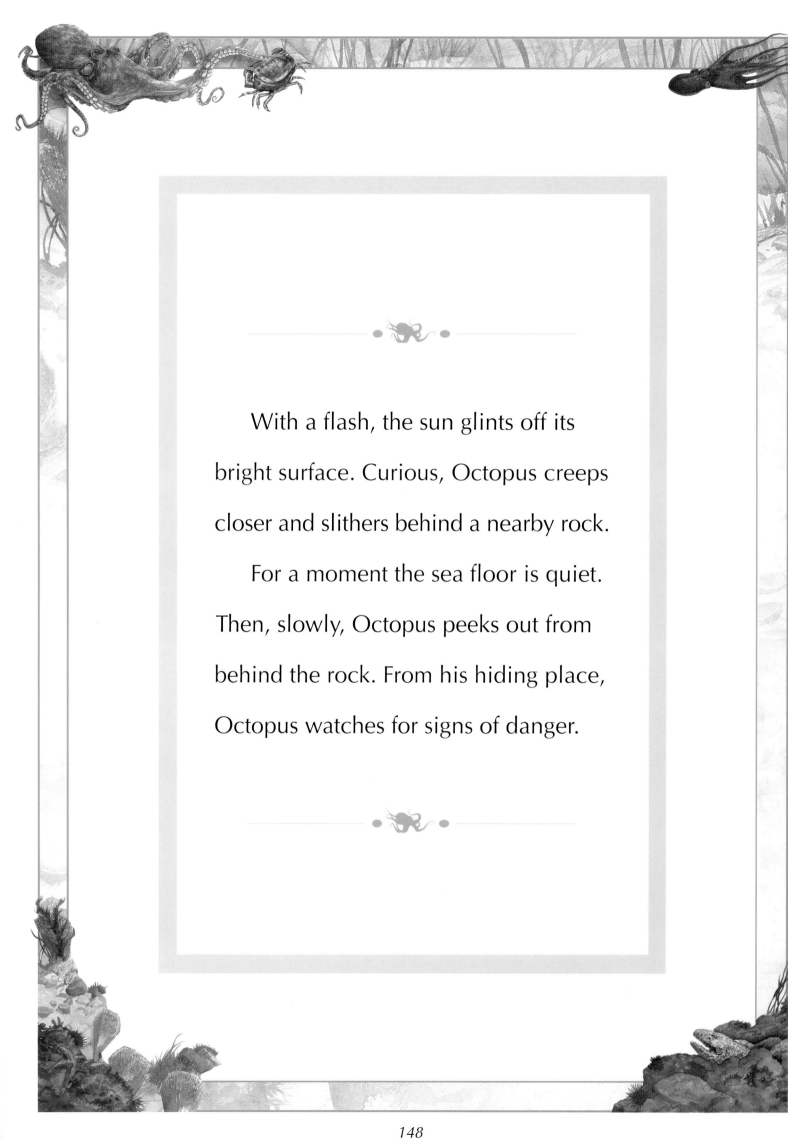

With a flash, the sun glints off its
bright surface. Curious, Octopus creeps
closer and slithers behind a nearby rock.

For a moment the sea floor is quiet.
Then, slowly, Octopus peeks out from
behind the rock. From his hiding place,
Octopus watches for signs of danger.

When he is sure it is safe, Octopus snakes an arm toward the piece of glass and snatches it. For a moment he investigates with the suckers on his arms, tasting the new object and feeling its shiny-smooth surface.

Then, Octopus backs away from his hiding place and heads toward home. The slender tip of one of his arms is still wrapped tightly around the shining piece of glass. It will soon become a part of his collection.

But before he reaches his safe den, Octopus spies danger. From between two rocks, a hungry moray eel strikes. Octopus' body turns dark and he squirts a cloud of ink at the eel. The eel attacks the cloud. It doesn't see Octopus shoot off in the opposite direction. Octopus changes color again, this time to a sandy shade of gray, and rockets behind a stony outcropping.

The eel is confused by the ink. It cannot smell Octopus. It bursts through the cloud and glides right over him.

The eel disappears into the distance, and Octopus begins to rise toward a hole in a rocky undersea cliff—his home.

Just as he is about to slide into the hidden rock-hole, he sees that something else is there. A larger octopus has moved in. The big octopus is wedged tightly into the hole, sitting on shells and rocks that Octopus collected.

The intruder reaches a huge arm toward Octopus, warning him to stay away. Octopus obeys. He will have to find a new home.

Octopus returns to the sea floor in search of a new shelter. The shiny piece of glass is tightly clasped in one of his busy, squirming arms. His other arms reach into crevices, feeling for a place to hide. They feel beneath coral and rocks, around corners and through holes, looking for a home.

As he crawls across the sea floor, his light brown body camouflages him well against the sand.

The sun's rays begin to grow dim. A seahorse floats in the still water, its tail twisted around a stalk of green seaweed. Octopus moves past it, brushing the seaweed with his long arm and jiggling the seahorse around.

Another arm reaches over a huge gray rock. A third snakes around it. There, hidden beneath the giant rock, Octopus discovers a hiding place.

Octopus pours his body through the tiny

opening and explores the cave beneath. It

is just the right size—too small for an eel

or grouper, but perfect for a flexible octopus.

Octopus is satisfied that he has found a safe

shelter and begins his house cleaning.

Octopus squirts water from his funnel,

blowing pebbles and shells out the tiny

doorway. Finally, the den is clear, ready for

Octopus to move in.

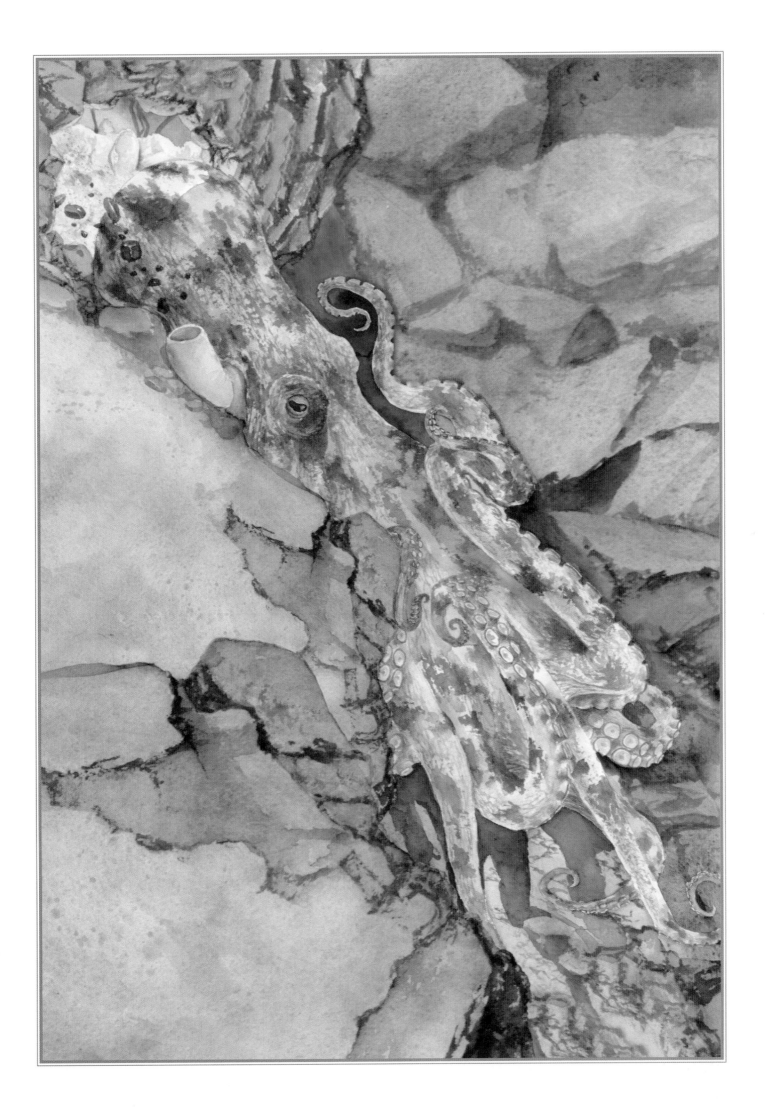

Next, Octopus builds a fence. With his front arms, he sweeps gravel away from the hole to make a little clearing. Then he gathers materials and cleans them. Jagged and smooth pieces of rock, empty clamshells, broken coral and the sparkling piece of glass all become part of a fence for Octopus.

Finally, Octopus' home is complete. As night comes, he slips inside.

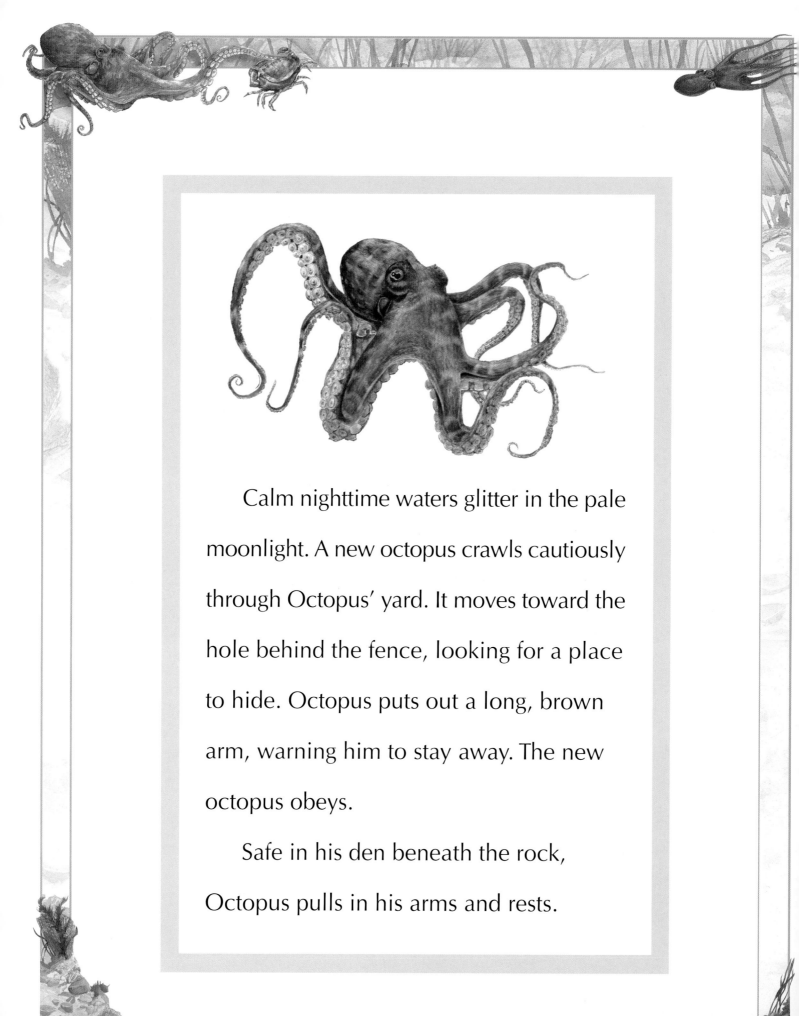

Calm nighttime waters glitter in the pale moonlight. A new octopus crawls cautiously through Octopus' yard. It moves toward the hole behind the fence, looking for a place to hide. Octopus puts out a long, brown arm, warning him to stay away. The new octopus obeys.

Safe in his den beneath the rock, Octopus pulls in his arms and rests.

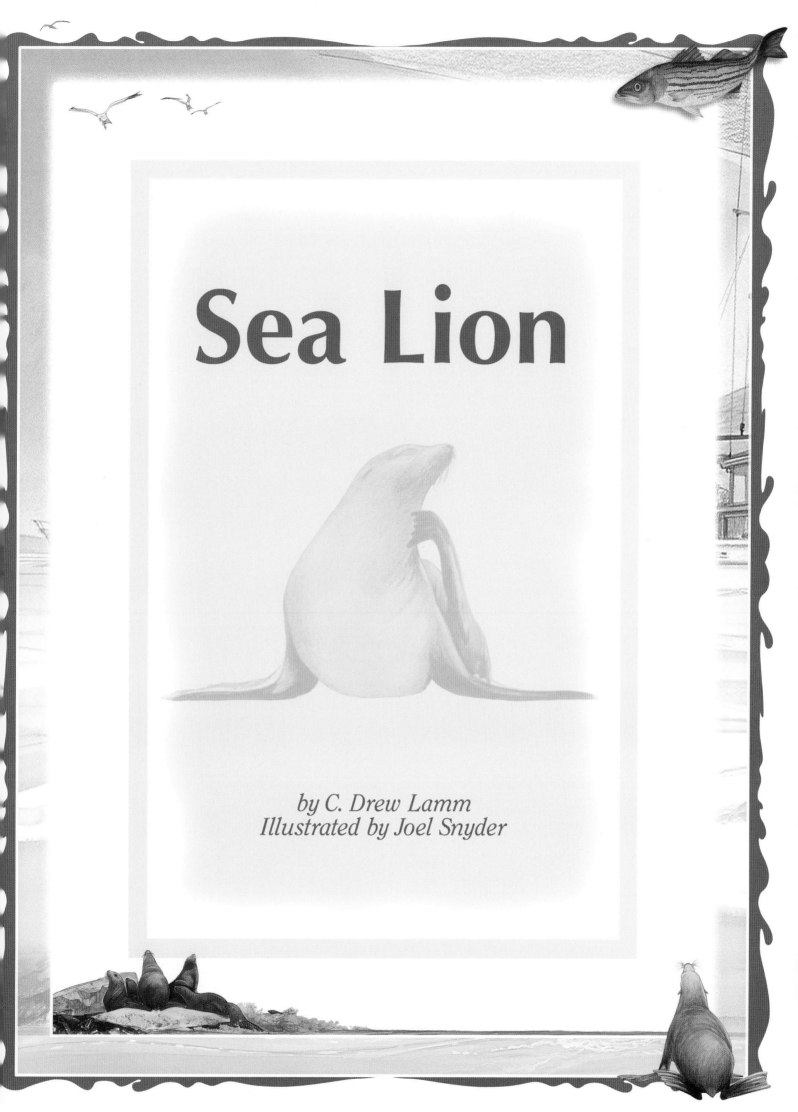

Sea Lion

by C. Drew Lamm
Illustrated by Joel Snyder

Today is Sea Lion's first birthday. He's a yearling. As he pushes his way through the roar of sea lions on the beach where he was born, a large male charges down the sand. Sea Lion lopes out of his path. He reaches his mother, but she nudges him away. She has just given birth. She smells her new pup to recognize it among the hundreds of others on the beach. They bark back and forth, learning each other's distinct voices.

Soon Mother will swim out to sea to forage for food. When she returns, she'll find her new pup by its smell and its voice, just as she found Sea Lion the year before.

Sea Lion sees a rumble of males heading out to the ocean. These males are looking for a new place to haul out with plenty of food. Sea Lion leaves home and follows them up the coast of California.

Late in the afternoon, Sea Lion hears an alarm bark. He spots a dark shape in the water and hurries toward shore. Sea Lion and the rest of the males leap ten feet up onto a rock ledge. Below them a great white shark streaks past.

It's hot on the rocks, and Sea Lion sticks a flipper up in the air to cool off.

When all seems still, the sea lions leap off the rocks. They dive, chasing after fish and other tasty treats.

As night sets, the sea lions close in together. They float as a large "raft." Sea Lion makes sucking sounds with his mouth as he used to do when he nestled with his mother.

As the rising sun glitters across the ocean, Sea Lion wakes hungry. Diving, he flies through the water toward a fish caught in an abandoned net. Sea Lion dives, mouth open and…

He feels something loop around his neck. He lashes to the right. The left. He dives. It tightens. He's caught in the net, too.

Sea Lion struggles until he's limp. The fishing net cuts into him and pinches his neck. He can't breathe well.

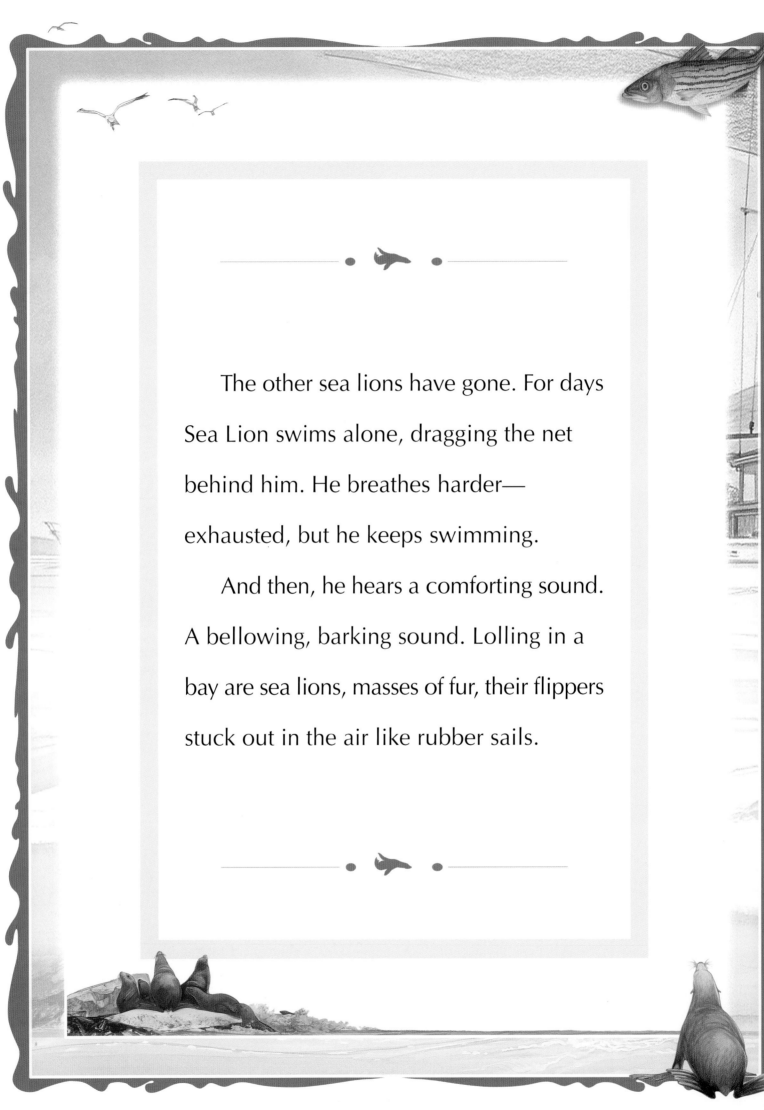

The other sea lions have gone. For days Sea Lion swims alone, dragging the net behind him. He breathes harder— exhausted, but he keeps swimming.

And then, he hears a comforting sound. A bellowing, barking sound. Lolling in a bay are sea lions, masses of fur, their flippers stuck out in the air like rubber sails.

Beyond them are more sea lions, lumped on floating docks. Sea Lion pulls himself up onto one of the docks.

A large male snorts and knocks Sea Lion off with a sweep of his head. Sea Lion leaps up again. He lands on another snoozing male. This one moans and rolls over. Sea Lion collapses beside him.

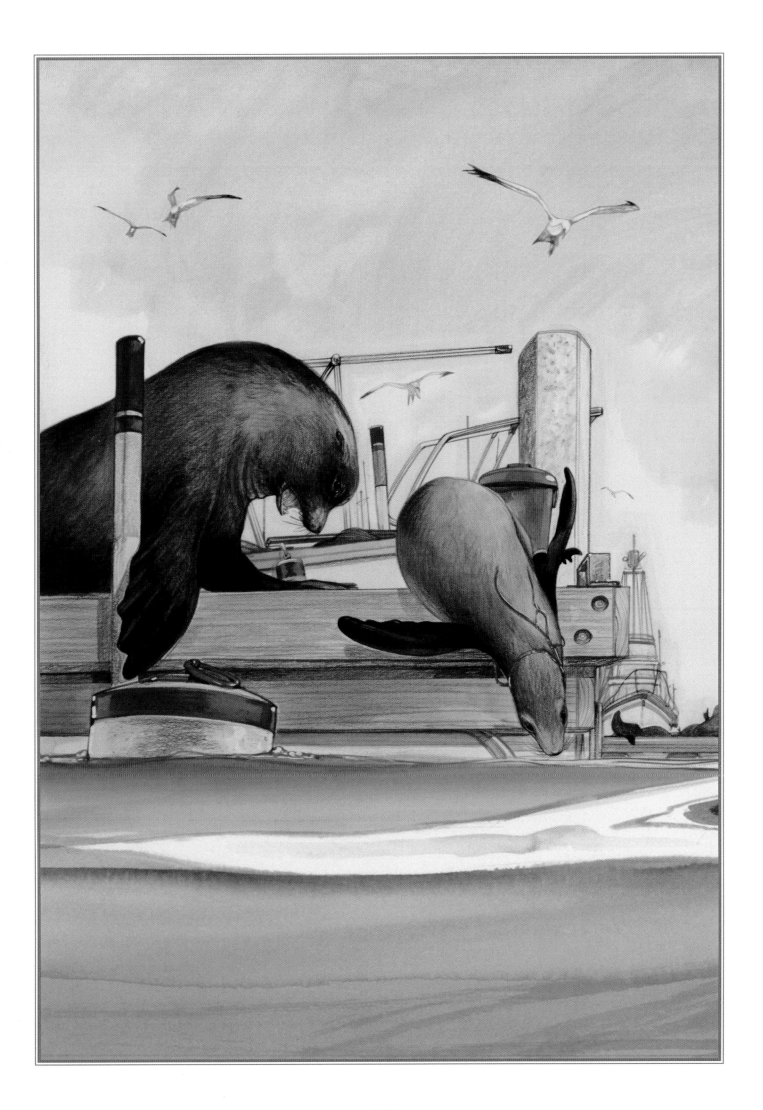

Sea Lion needs a quiet place to try and rest. He swims to an empty dock and drags himself up again.

A ferry chugs into the bay. He hears its horn. Sea gulls fly around him. He hears their calls. On the docks all around him, sea lions roar and groan. And then a new sound—a soft roar over the commotion. Is it danger? Sea Lion tries to lift his head.

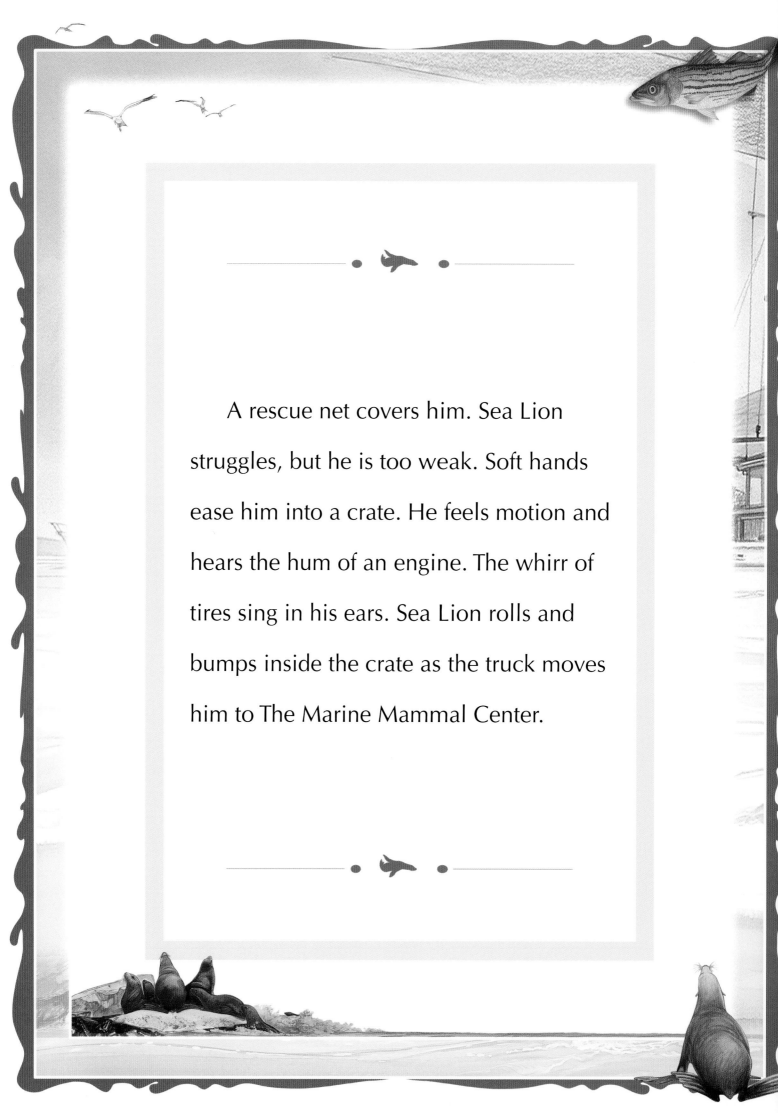

A rescue net covers him. Sea Lion struggles, but he is too weak. Soft hands ease him into a crate. He feels motion and hears the hum of an engine. The whirr of tires sing in his ears. Sea Lion rolls and bumps inside the crate as the truck moves him to The Marine Mammal Center.

Once there, gentle hands remove the fishing net around Sea Lion's neck. Each day he is brought fish to eat, and his wound is washed. As he becomes stronger, he barks bubbles and slowly begins to twirl and leap.

When Sea Lion is well, he is loaded onto the truck again and driven to a quiet shore. He's free.

Once again in the ocean, Sea Lion soars and dives, rolls and spins. He swims back to the docks and pulls himself out of the water.

Now it is time to play "King of the Dock." Sea Lion lunges and bumps off two large males. Another male slams him in the chest and nips his neck. Sea Lion opens his mouth, hits and shoves. The male somersaults off the dock.

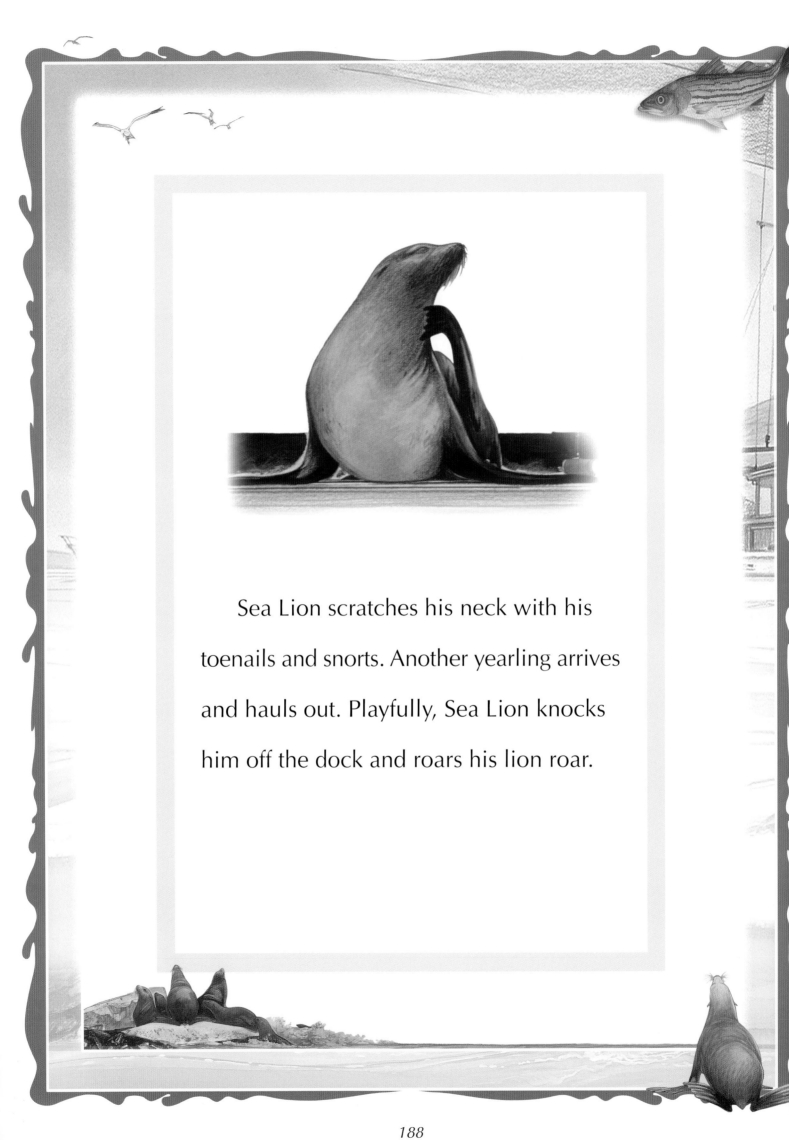

Sea Lion scratches his neck with his toenails and snorts. Another yearling arrives and hauls out. Playfully, Sea Lion knocks him off the dock and roars his lion roar.

Lobster

by Kathleen Hollenbeck
Illustrated by Jon Weiman

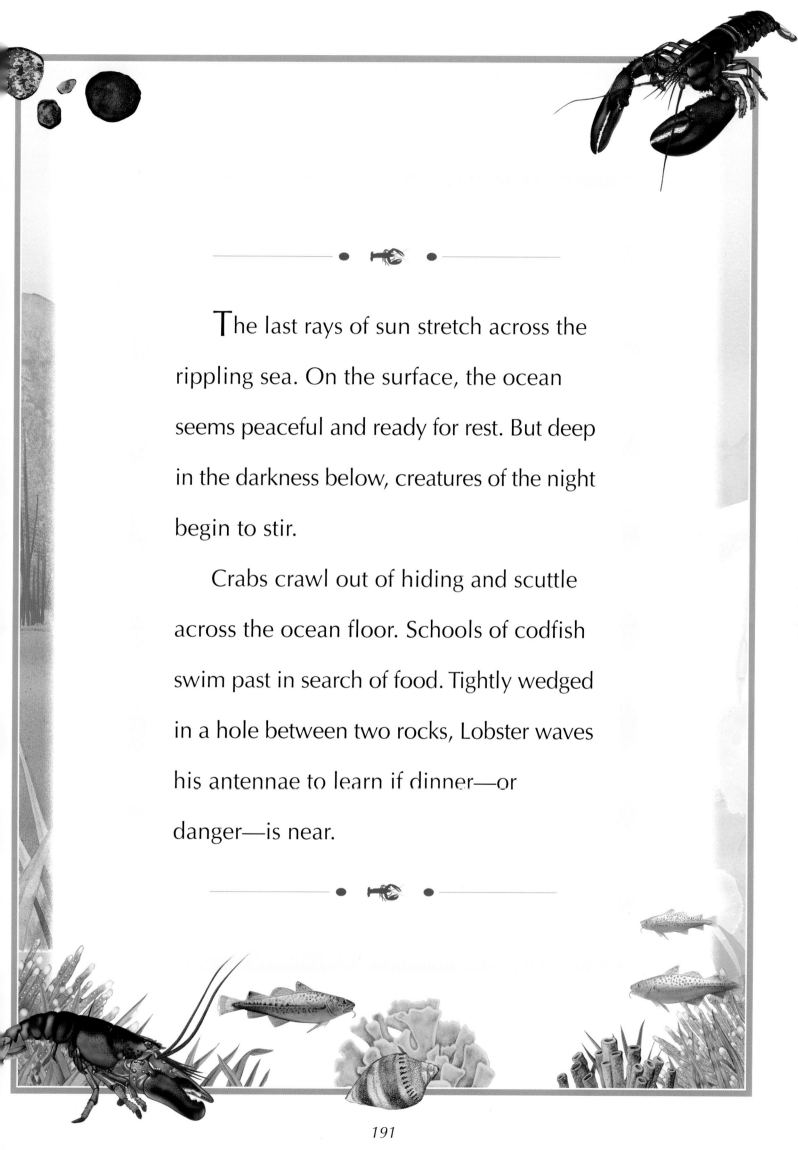

The last rays of sun stretch across the rippling sea. On the surface, the ocean seems peaceful and ready for rest. But deep in the darkness below, creatures of the night begin to stir.

Crabs crawl out of hiding and scuttle across the ocean floor. Schools of codfish swim past in search of food. Tightly wedged in a hole between two rocks, Lobster waves his antennae to learn if dinner—or danger—is near.

His antennae sense chemicals in the
water coming from a tasty meal nearby.
Hungry, Lobster crawls out of his hole.

Without warning, a codfish darts out
of the blackness. Lobster pulls back into
his den. He struggles, trying to draw his
giant claws inside. As Lobster disappears,
the codfish lunges.

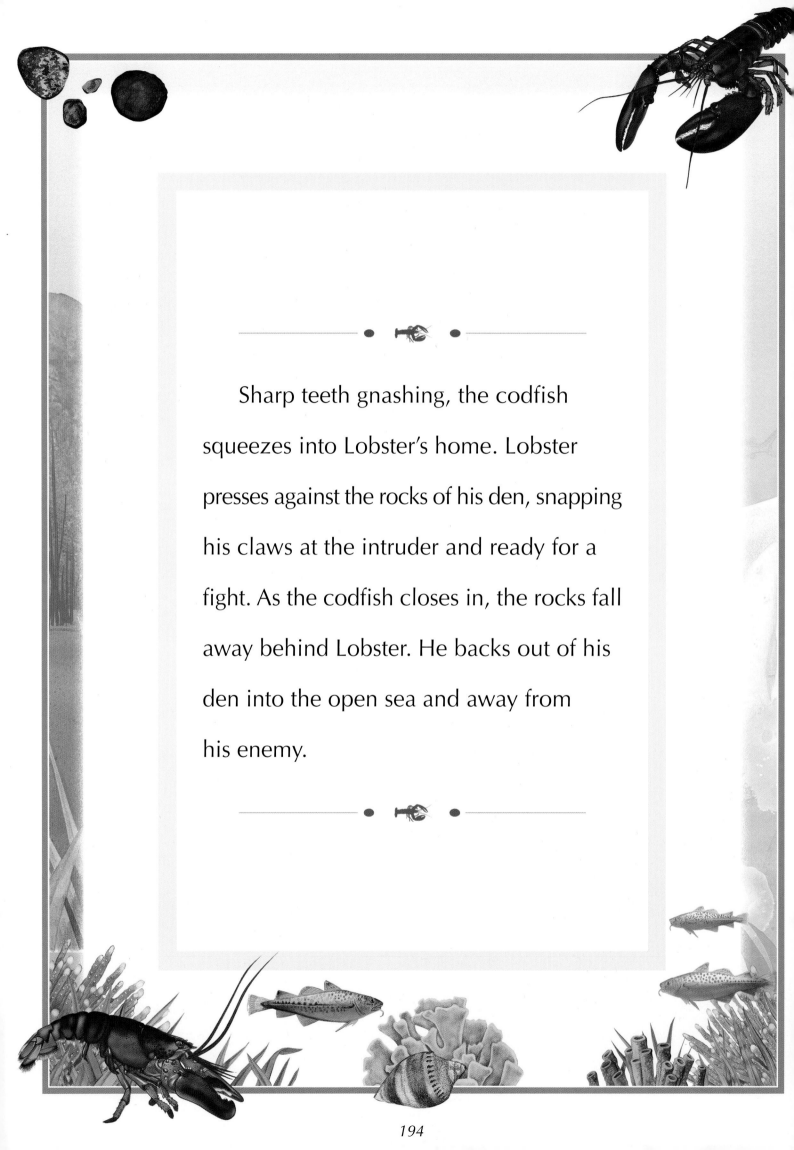

Sharp teeth gnashing, the codfish squeezes into Lobster's home. Lobster presses against the rocks of his den, snapping his claws at the intruder and ready for a fight. As the codfish closes in, the rocks fall away behind Lobster. He backs out of his den into the open sea and away from his enemy.

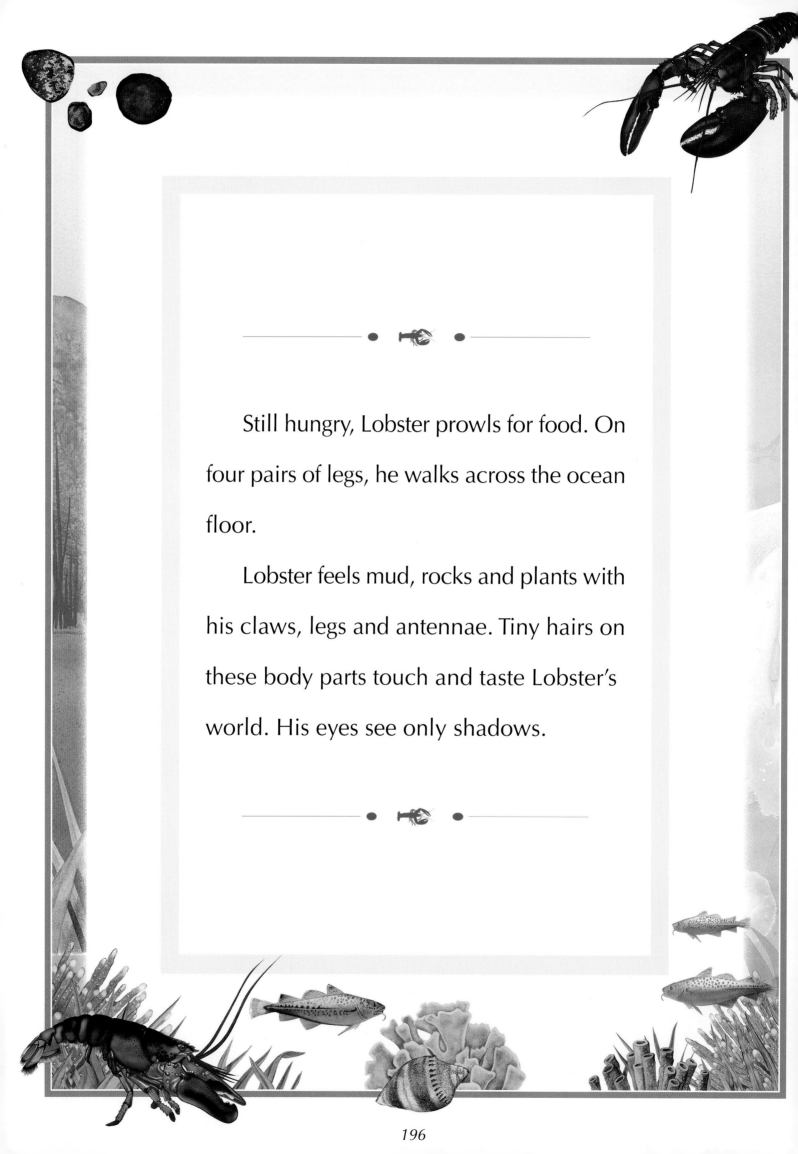

Still hungry, Lobster prowls for food. On four pairs of legs, he walks across the ocean floor.

Lobster feels mud, rocks and plants with his claws, legs and antennae. Tiny hairs on these body parts touch and taste Lobster's world. His eyes see only shadows.

Finally, Lobster finds his prey. A red rock crab raises its claws, ready for battle. Lobster seizes the crab in his largest claw. Boldly, the crab swings its own claws, trying to break free. But the crab's tiny claws are no match for Lobster's mighty ones.

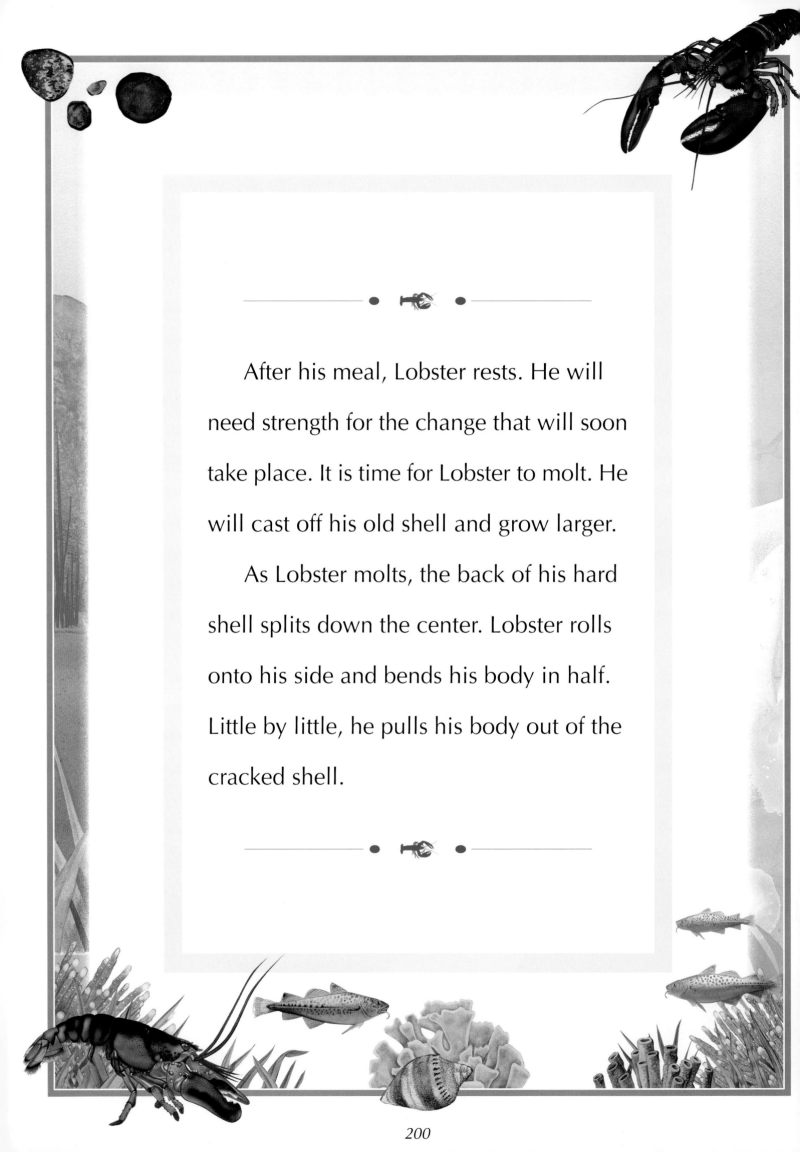

After his meal, Lobster rests. He will need strength for the change that will soon take place. It is time for Lobster to molt. He will cast off his old shell and grow larger.

As Lobster molts, the back of his hard shell splits down the center. Lobster rolls onto his side and bends his body in half. Little by little, he pulls his body out of the cracked shell.

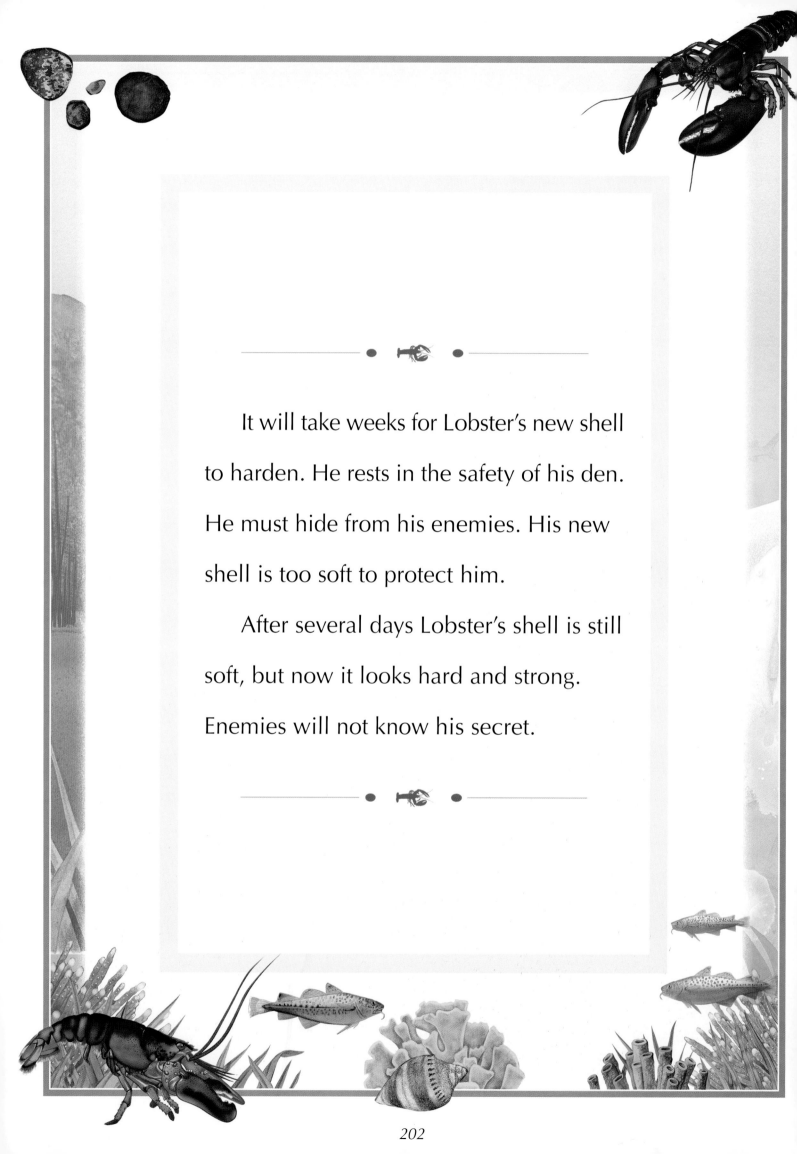

It will take weeks for Lobster's new shell to harden. He rests in the safety of his den. He must hide from his enemies. His new shell is too soft to protect him.

After several days Lobster's shell is still soft, but now it looks hard and strong. Enemies will not know his secret.

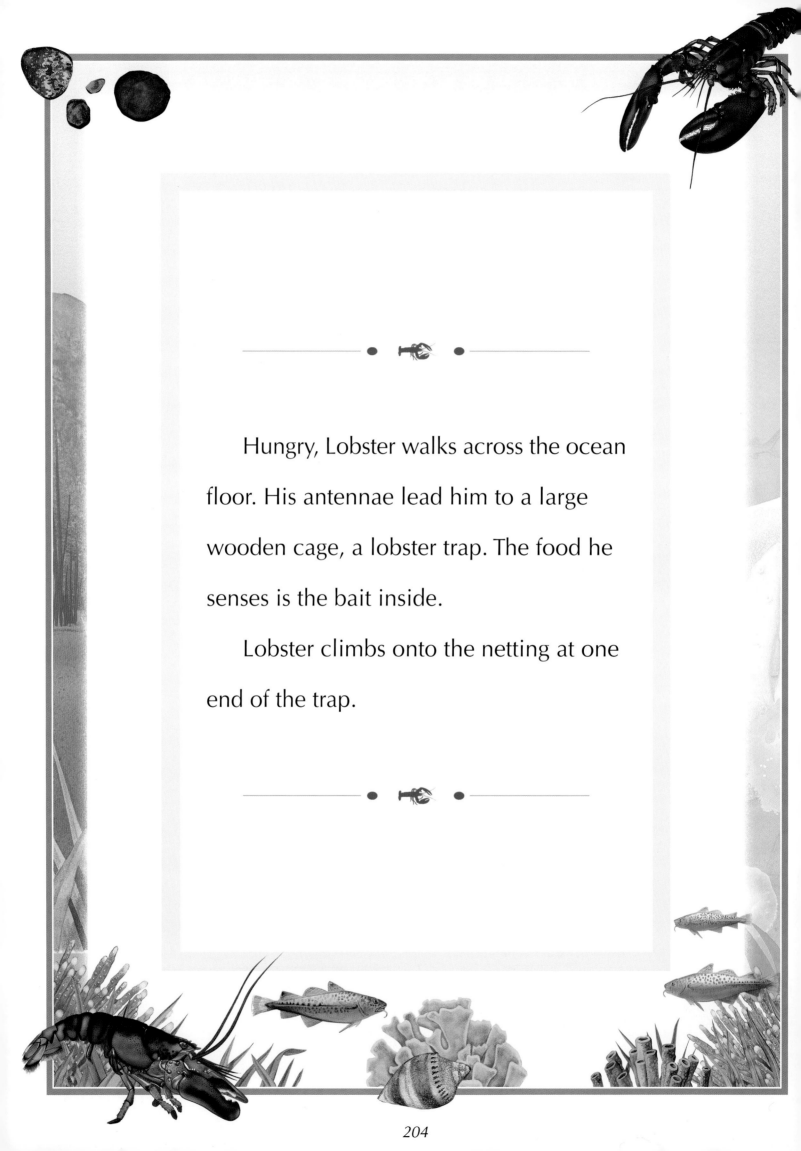

Hungry, Lobster walks across the ocean floor. His antennae lead him to a large wooden cage, a lobster trap. The food he senses is the bait inside.

Lobster climbs onto the netting at one end of the trap.

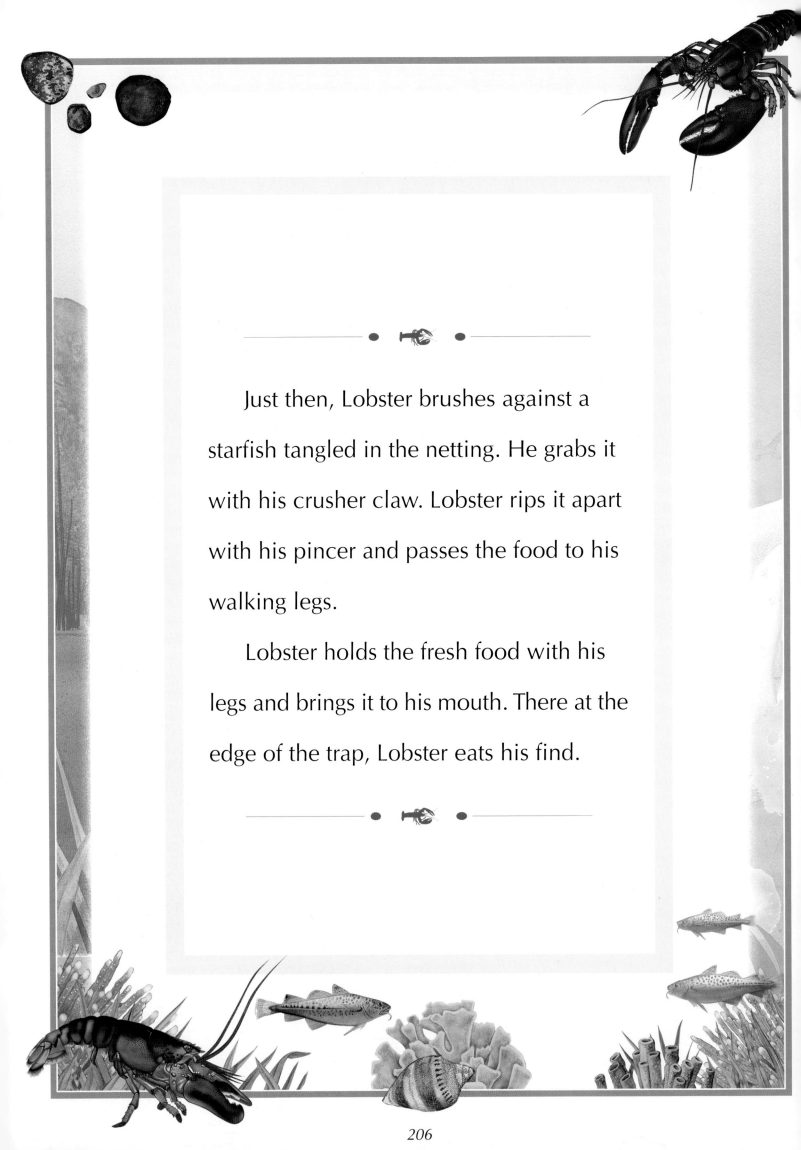

Just then, Lobster brushes against a starfish tangled in the netting. He grabs it with his crusher claw. Lobster rips it apart with his pincer and passes the food to his walking legs.

Lobster holds the fresh food with his legs and brings it to his mouth. There at the edge of the trap, Lobster eats his find.

Lobster's antennae still sense the tasty bait, but he is satisfied. He steps back onto the ocean floor. Suddenly a huge fish lunges at him. Lobster jumps up. He thrusts his antennae back over his head, and draws his walking legs in toward his body. Rapidly flexing his tail, he speeds backward through the water.

Lobster's eyes face backward as he races. They help him find a hole among boulders and he slips in easily. Snapping his claws fiercely, Lobster warns the fish to stay away.

The fish gives up and Lobster is alone. Soon night ends on the ocean floor. Crabs, codfish and other night creatures rest in the shelter of rocks or plants.

Safe in his hideaway, Lobster waits for night to come again. In a few weeks, Lobster's shell will be truly hard and strong. But for now his secret must be kept safe from his enemies until he is once again a fierce and sturdy creature of the sea.

Harbor Seal

by Kathleen Weidner Zoehfeld
Illustrated by Lisa Bonforte

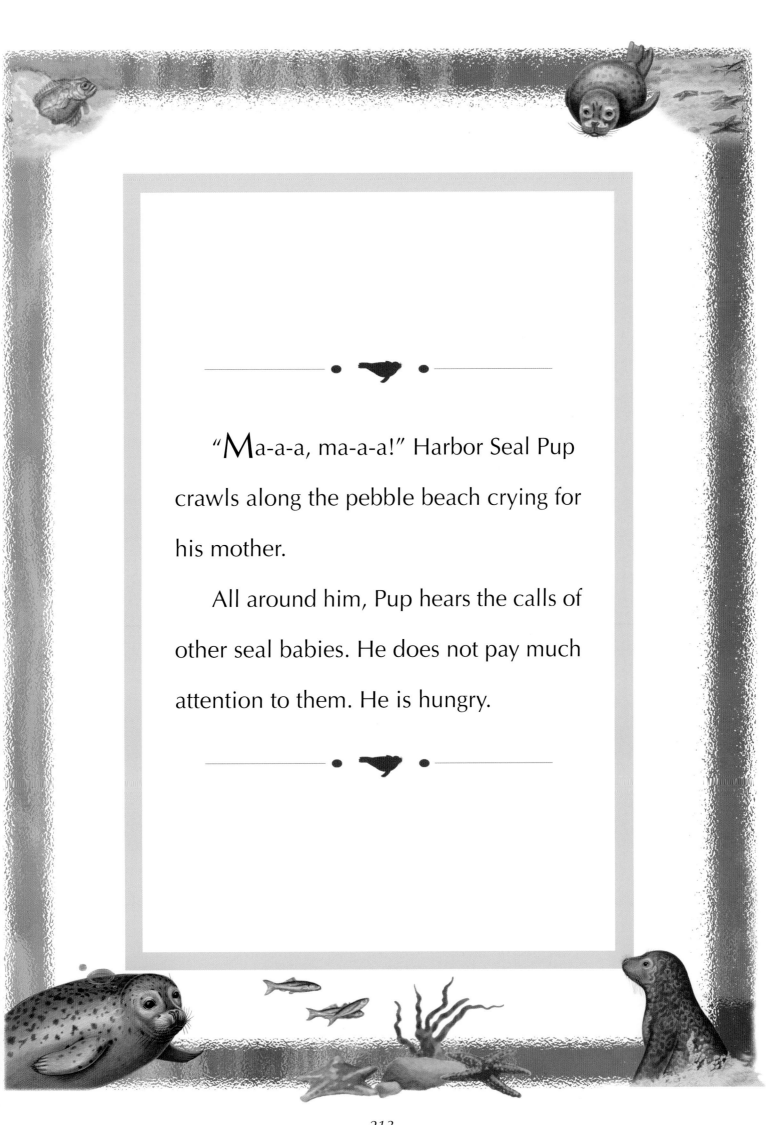

"Ma-a-a, ma-a-a!" Harbor Seal Pup crawls along the pebble beach crying for his mother.

All around him, Pup hears the calls of other seal babies. He does not pay much attention to them. He is hungry.

Not too far ahead, he sees a mother seal. He hurries to her and reaches his nose up to sniff her neck.

But she is another baby's mother, not his. He moves on, crying even louder. But Pup's mother is not far away.

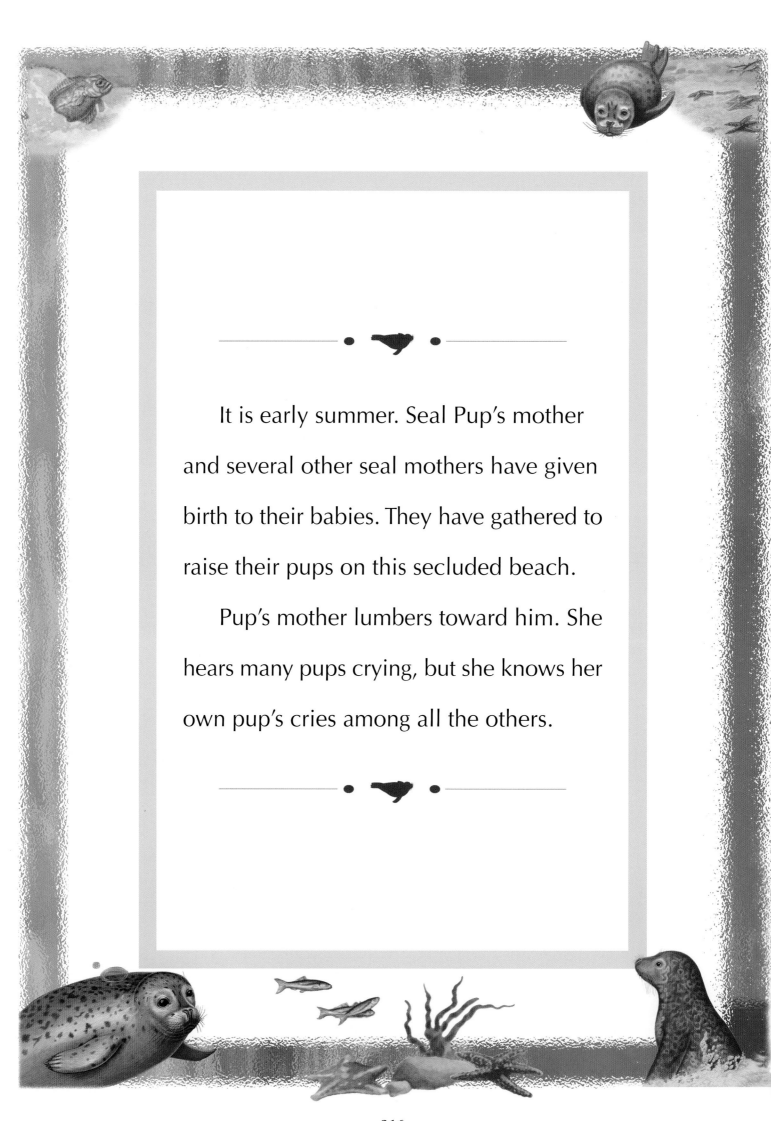

It is early summer. Seal Pup's mother and several other seal mothers have given birth to their babies. They have gathered to raise their pups on this secluded beach.

Pup's mother lumbers toward him. She hears many pups crying, but she knows her own pup's cries among all the others.

When she reaches him, she sniffs his neck. Pup's special scent tells his mother that this is really her baby. They touch noses.

Pup nuzzles her excitedly. Mother rolls over on her side and Pup begins to nurse. He drinks her rich milk.

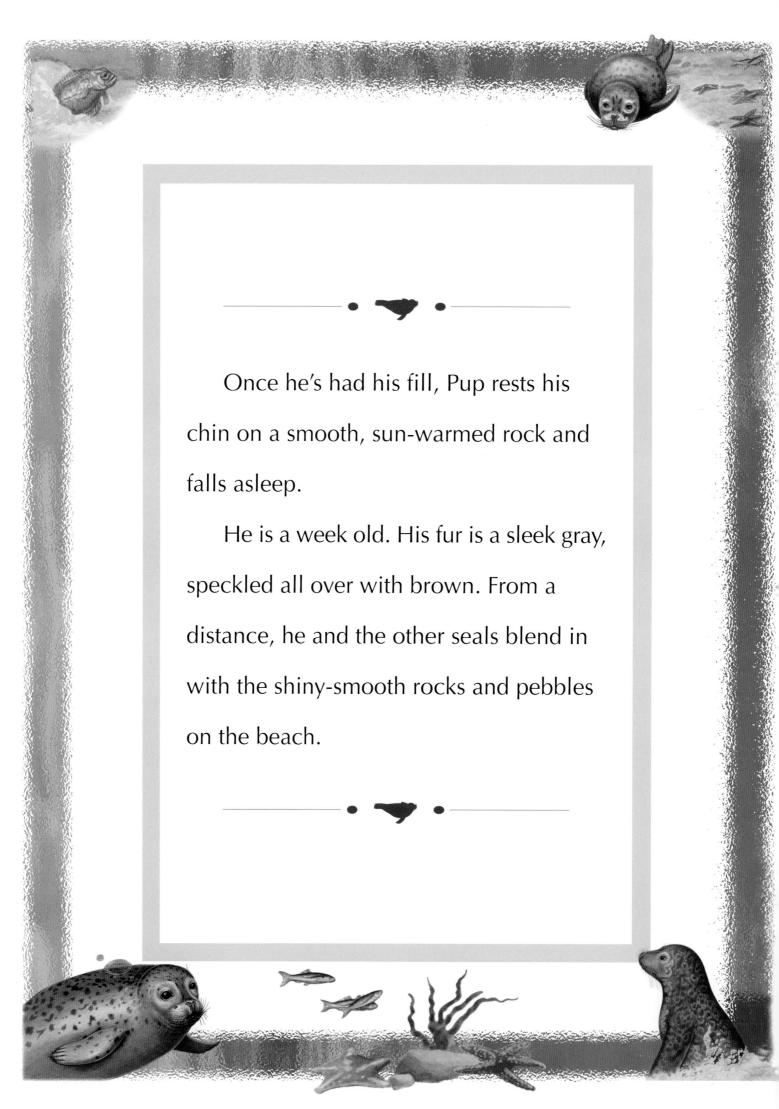

Once he's had his fill, Pup rests his chin on a smooth, sun-warmed rock and falls asleep.

He is a week old. His fur is a sleek gray, speckled all over with brown. From a distance, he and the other seals blend in with the shiny-smooth rocks and pebbles on the beach.

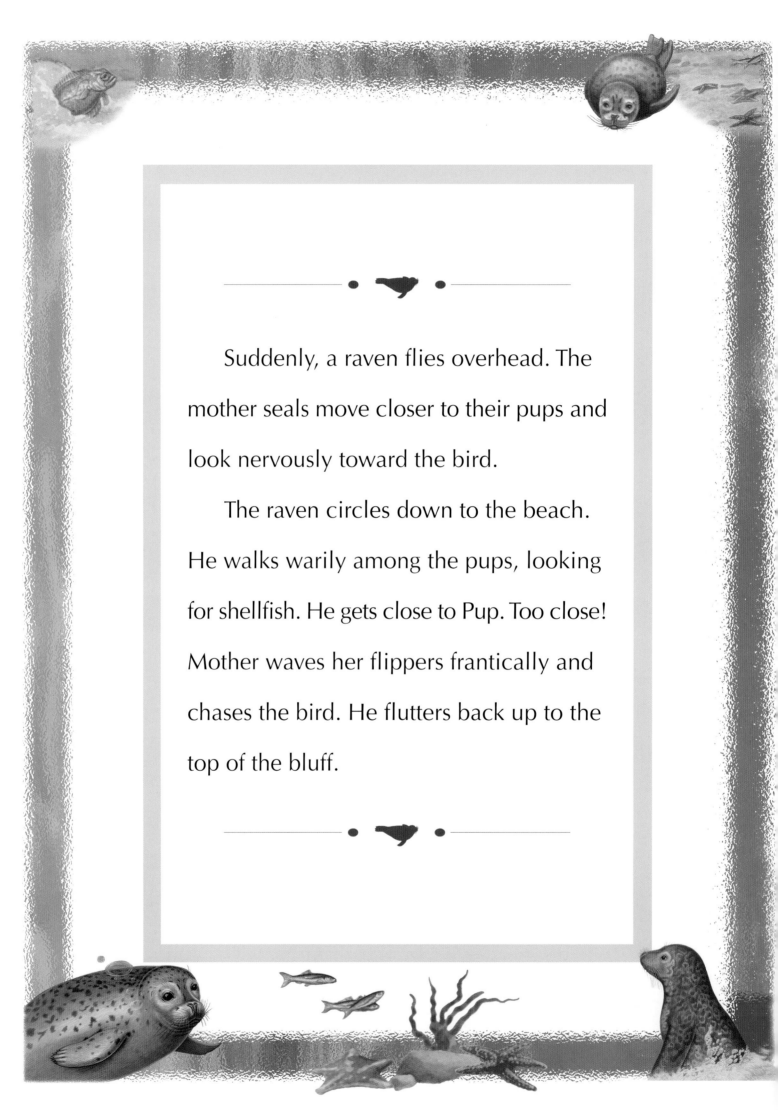

Suddenly, a raven flies overhead. The mother seals move closer to their pups and look nervously toward the bird.

The raven circles down to the beach. He walks warily among the pups, looking for shellfish. He gets close to Pup. Too close! Mother waves her flippers frantically and chases the bird. He flutters back up to the top of the bluff.

223

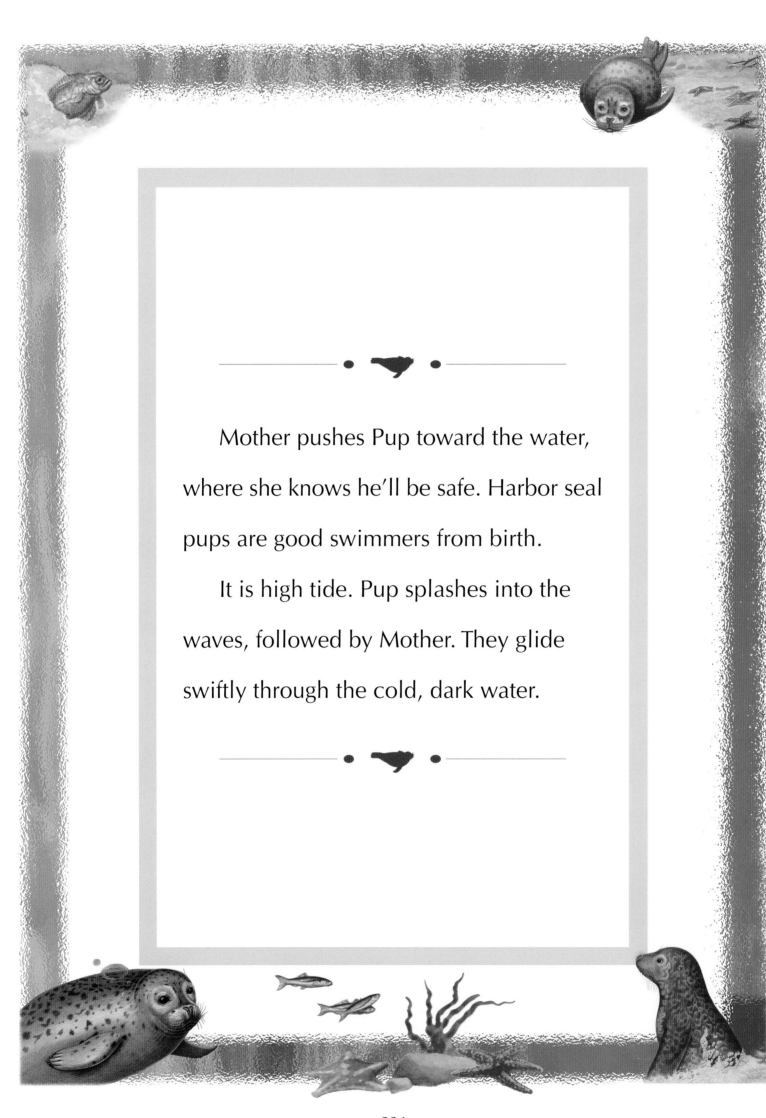

Mother pushes Pup toward the water, where she knows he'll be safe. Harbor seal pups are good swimmers from birth.

It is high tide. Pup splashes into the waves, followed by Mother. They glide swiftly through the cold, dark water.

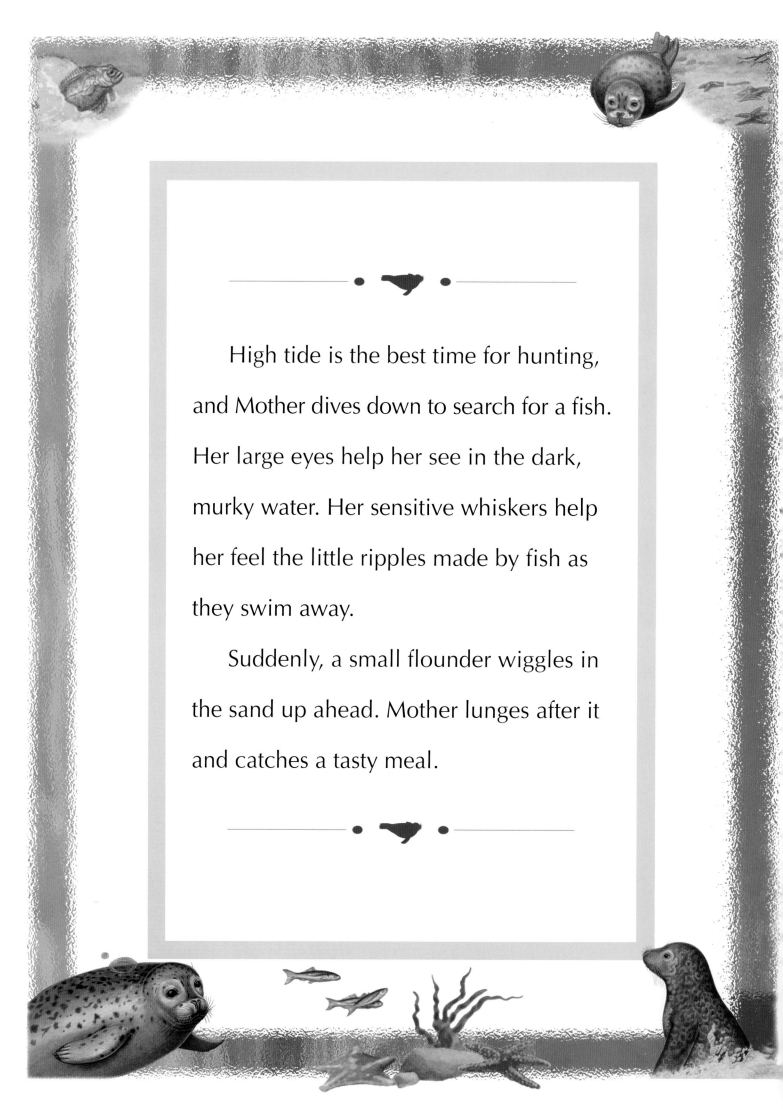

High tide is the best time for hunting, and Mother dives down to search for a fish. Her large eyes help her see in the dark, murky water. Her sensitive whiskers help her feel the little ripples made by fish as they swim away.

Suddenly, a small flounder wiggles in the sand up ahead. Mother lunges after it and catches a tasty meal.

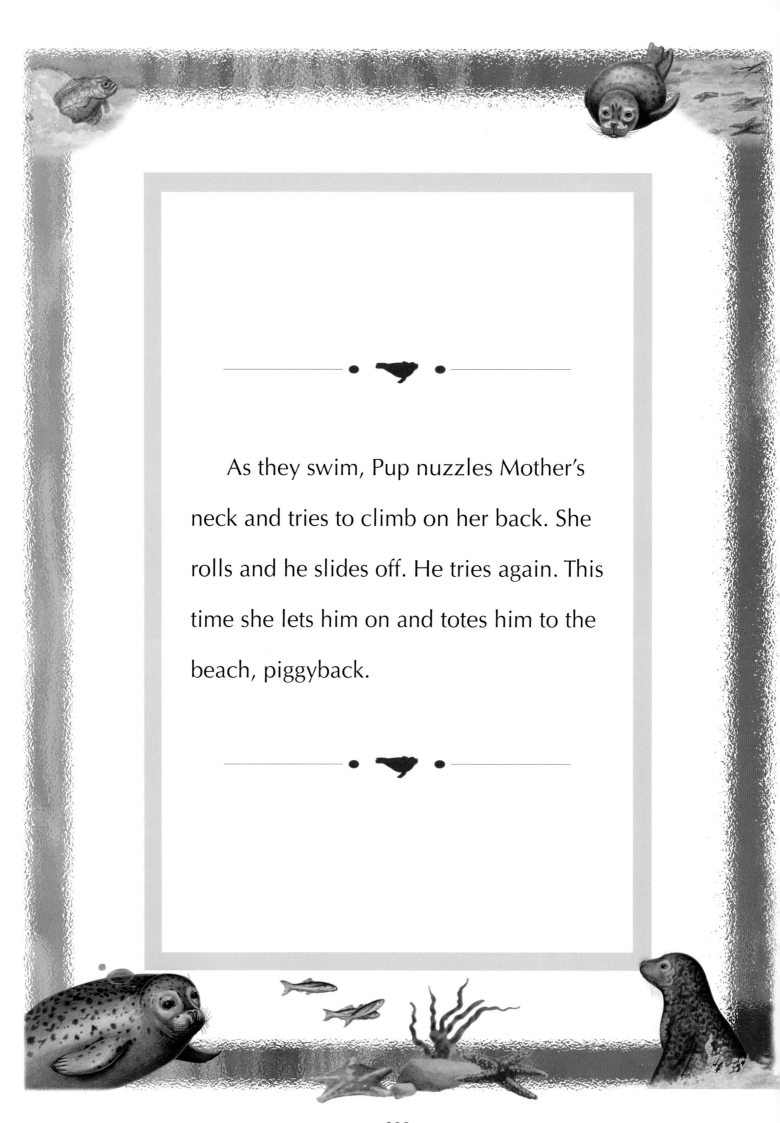

As they swim, Pup nuzzles Mother's neck and tries to climb on her back. She rolls and he slides off. He tries again. This time she lets him on and totes him to the beach, piggyback.

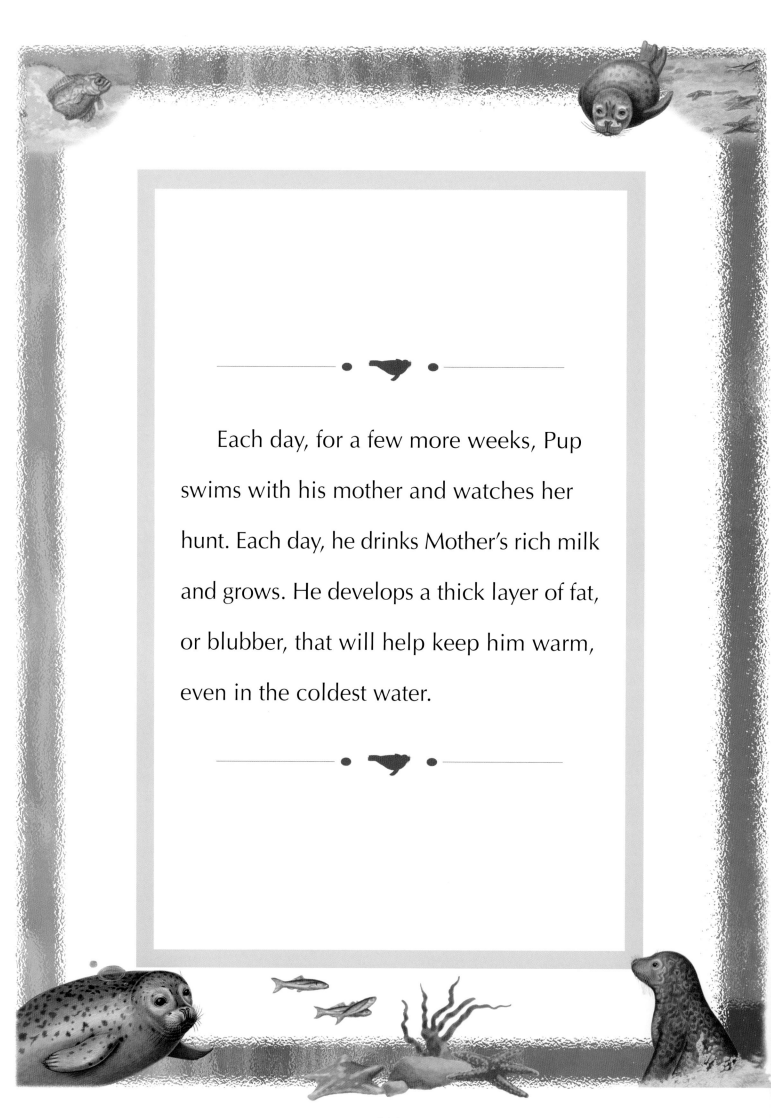

Each day, for a few more weeks, Pup
swims with his mother and watches her
hunt. Each day, he drinks Mother's rich milk
and grows. He develops a thick layer of fat,
or blubber, that will help keep him warm,
even in the coldest water.

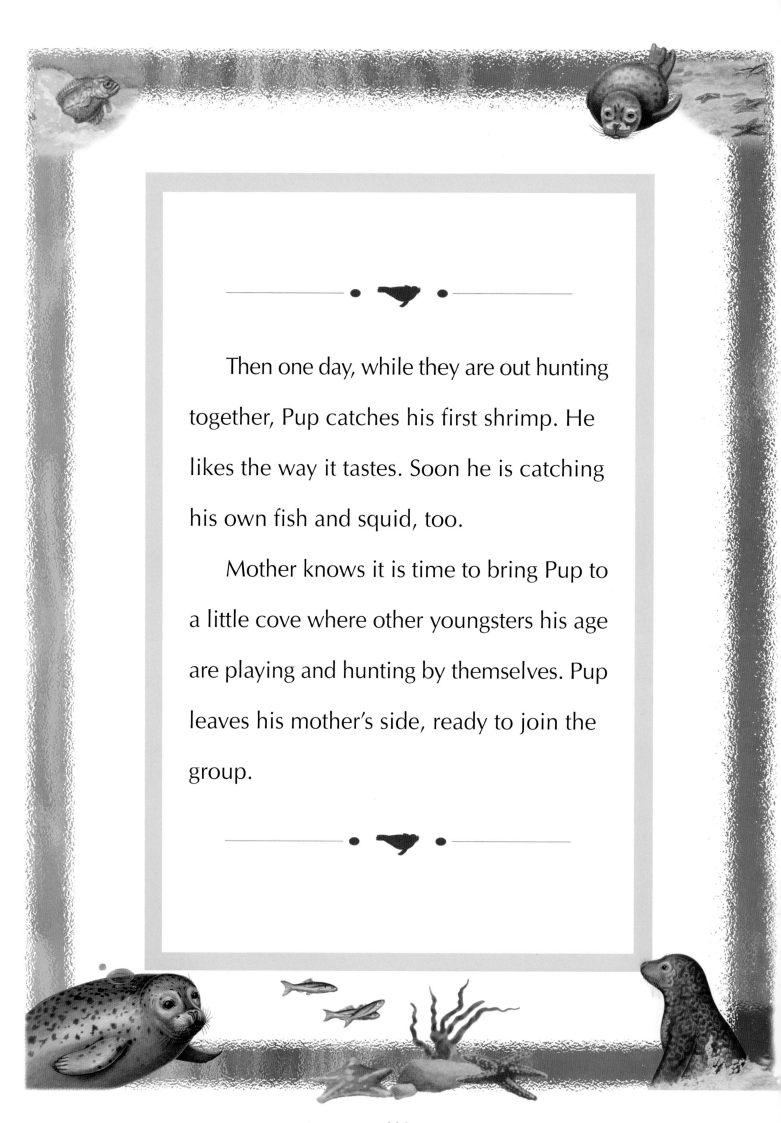

Then one day, while they are out hunting together, Pup catches his first shrimp. He likes the way it tastes. Soon he is catching his own fish and squid, too.

Mother knows it is time to bring Pup to a little cove where other youngsters his age are playing and hunting by themselves. Pup leaves his mother's side, ready to join the group.

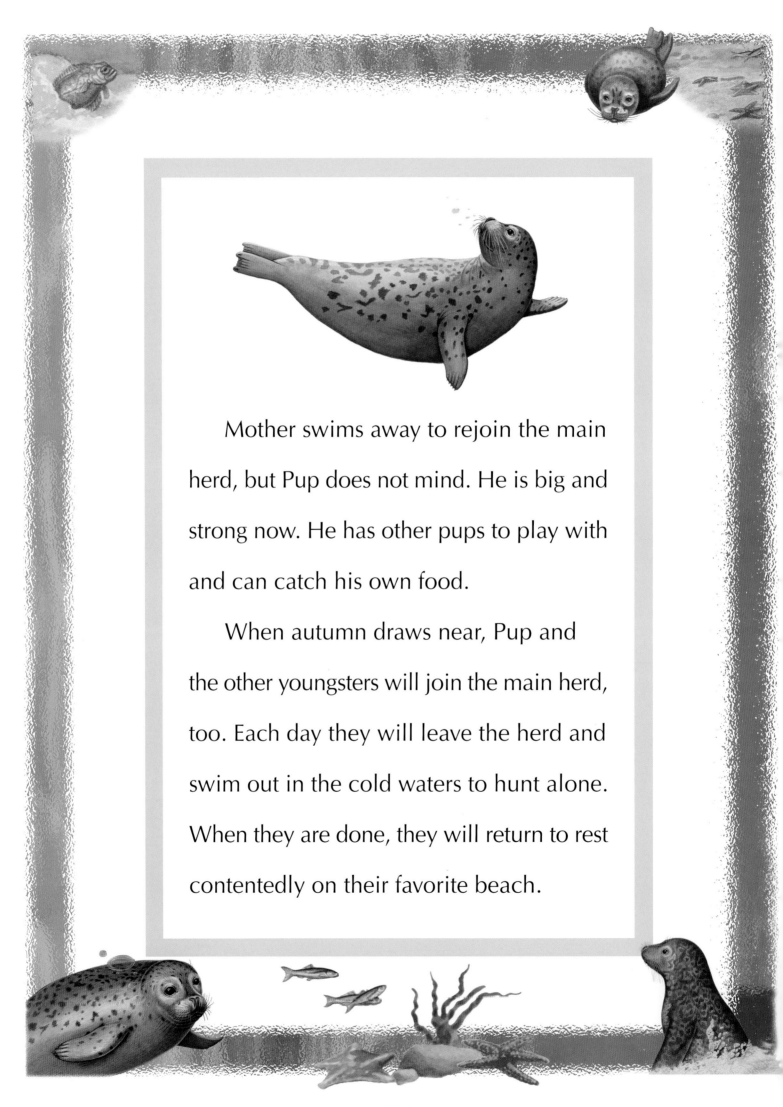

Mother swims away to rejoin the main herd, but Pup does not mind. He is big and strong now. He has other pups to play with and can catch his own food.

When autumn draws near, Pup and the other youngsters will join the main herd, too. Each day they will leave the herd and swim out in the cold waters to hunt alone. When they are done, they will return to rest contentedly on their favorite beach.

Orca

by Michael C. Armour
Illustrated by Katie Lee

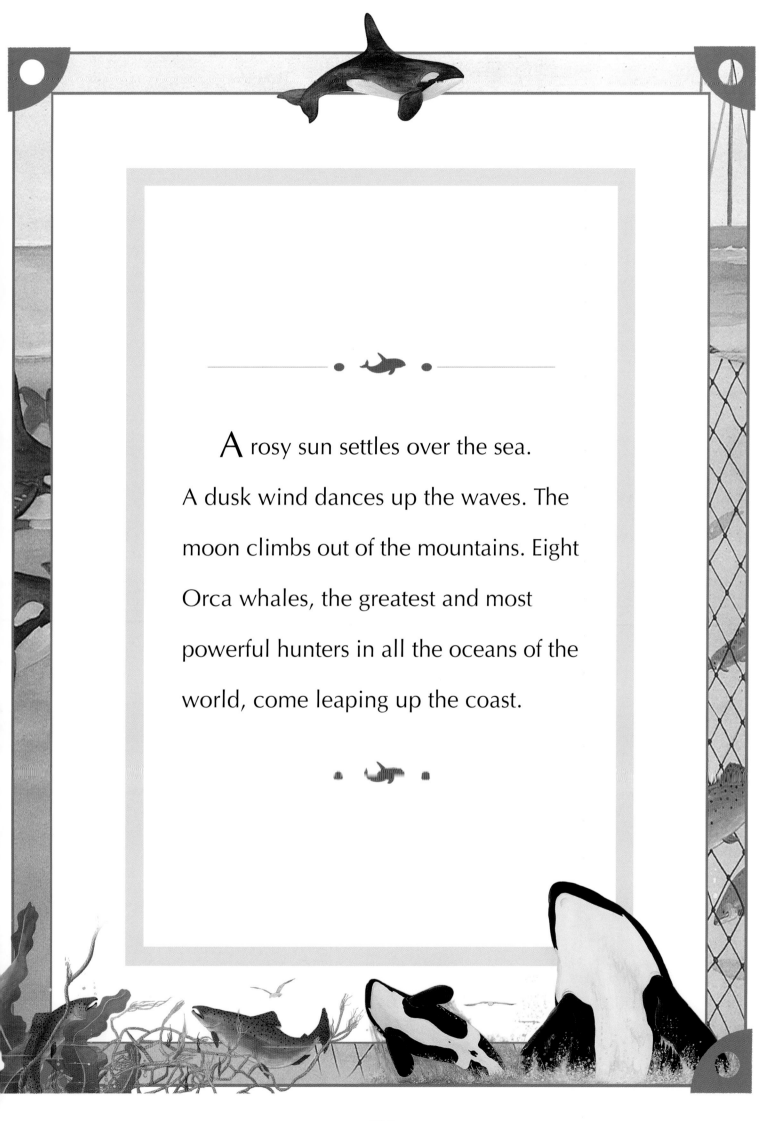

A rosy sun settles over the sea. A dusk wind dances up the waves. The moon climbs out of the mountains. Eight Orca whales, the greatest and most powerful hunters in all the oceans of the world, come leaping up the coast.

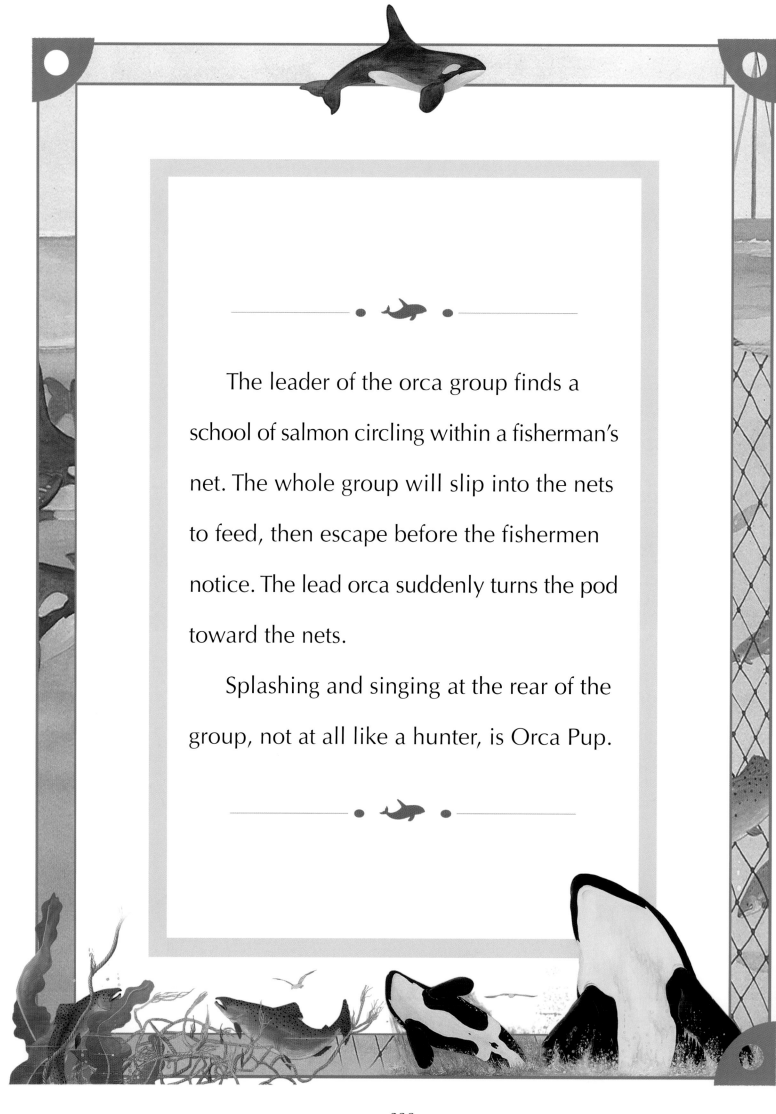

The leader of the orca group finds a school of salmon circling within a fisherman's net. The whole group will slip into the nets to feed, then escape before the fishermen notice. The lead orca suddenly turns the pod toward the nets.

Splashing and singing at the rear of the group, not at all like a hunter, is Orca Pup.

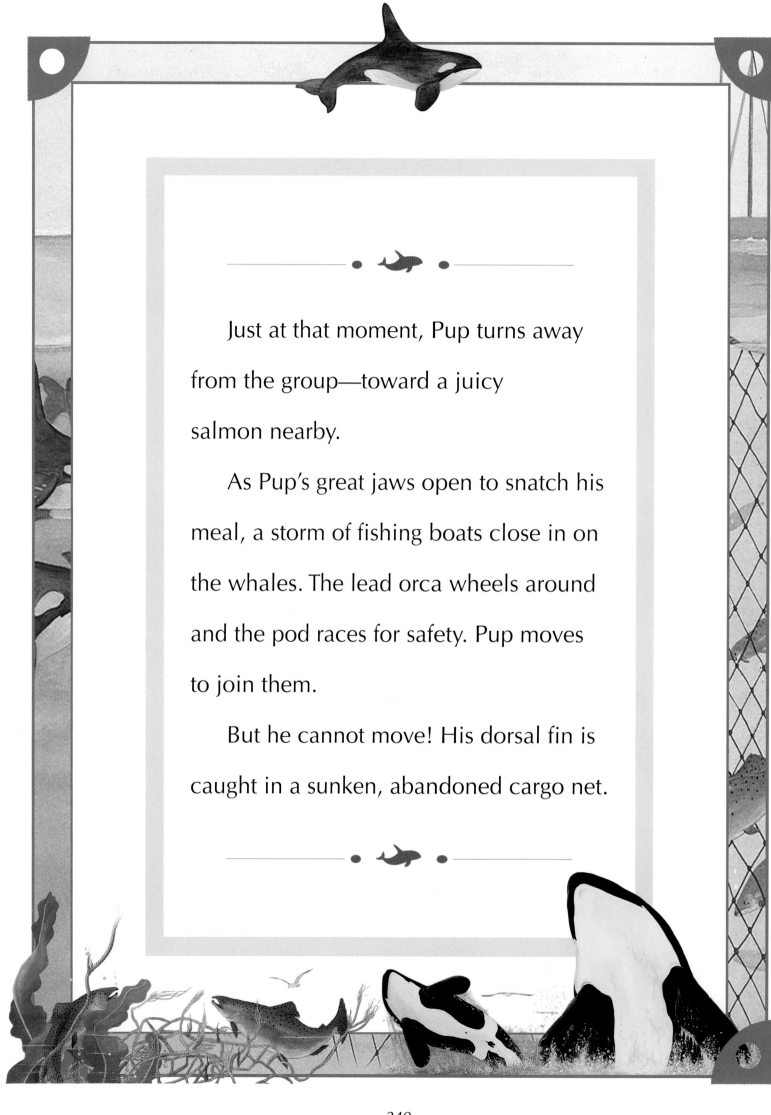

Just at that moment, Pup turns away
from the group—toward a juicy
salmon nearby.

As Pup's great jaws open to snatch his
meal, a storm of fishing boats close in on
the whales. The lead orca wheels around
and the pod races for safety. Pup moves
to join them.

But he cannot move! His dorsal fin is
caught in a sunken, abandoned cargo net.

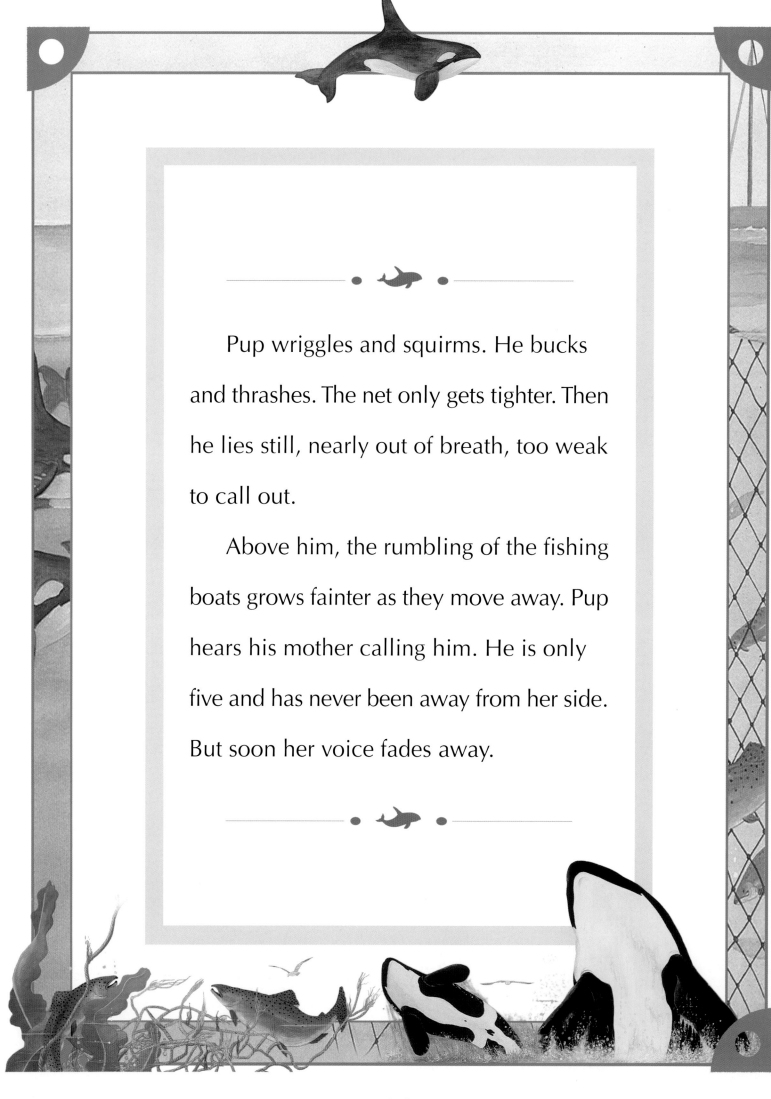

Pup wriggles and squirms. He bucks and thrashes. The net only gets tighter. Then he lies still, nearly out of breath, too weak to call out.

Above him, the rumbling of the fishing boats grows fainter as they move away. Pup hears his mother calling him. He is only five and has never been away from her side. But soon her voice fades away.

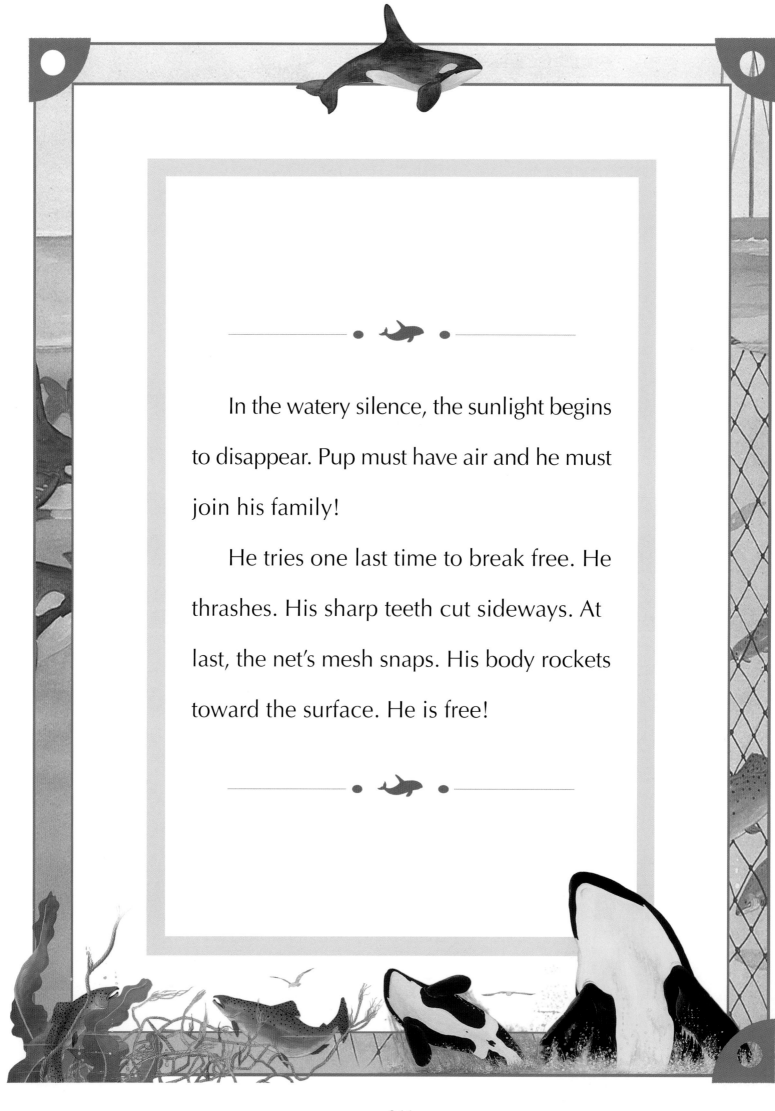

In the watery silence, the sunlight begins to disappear. Pup must have air and he must join his family!

He tries one last time to break free. He thrashes. His sharp teeth cut sideways. At last, the net's mesh snaps. His body rockets toward the surface. He is free!

Air! Night air rushes into his blowhole. His lungs fill like balloons.

But the fight has tired him. Alone and exhausted, Pup drifts half asleep through the lonely, moonlit seas…closer and closer to land.

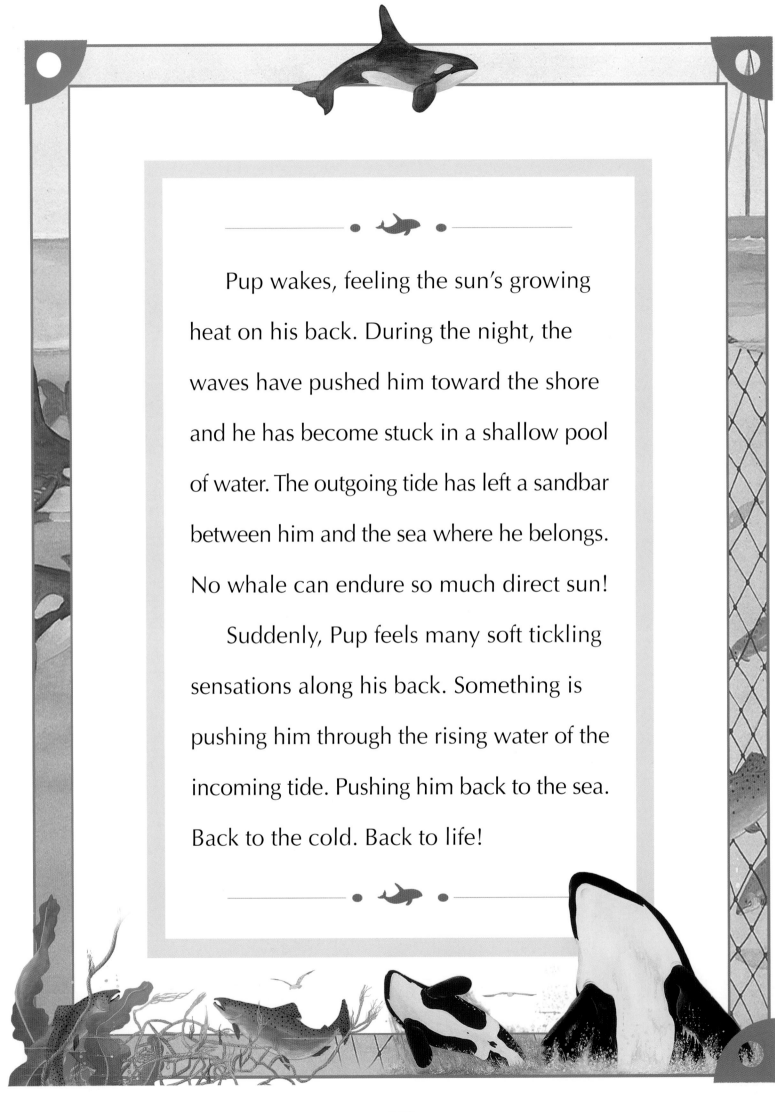

Pup wakes, feeling the sun's growing heat on his back. During the night, the waves have pushed him toward the shore and he has become stuck in a shallow pool of water. The outgoing tide has left a sandbar between him and the sea where he belongs. No whale can endure so much direct sun!

Suddenly, Pup feels many soft tickling sensations along his back. Something is pushing him through the rising water of the incoming tide. Pushing him back to the sea. Back to the cold. Back to life!

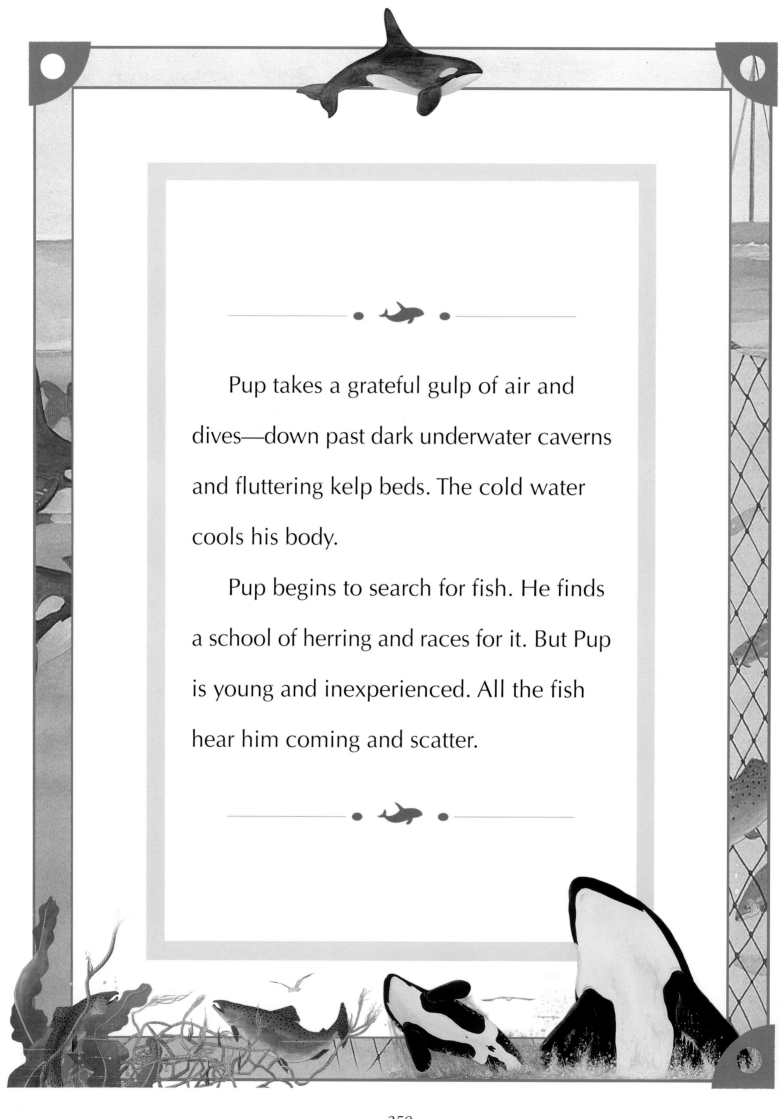

Pup takes a grateful gulp of air and dives—down past dark underwater caverns and fluttering kelp beds. The cold water cools his body.

Pup begins to search for fish. He finds a school of herring and races for it. But Pup is young and inexperienced. All the fish hear him coming and scatter.

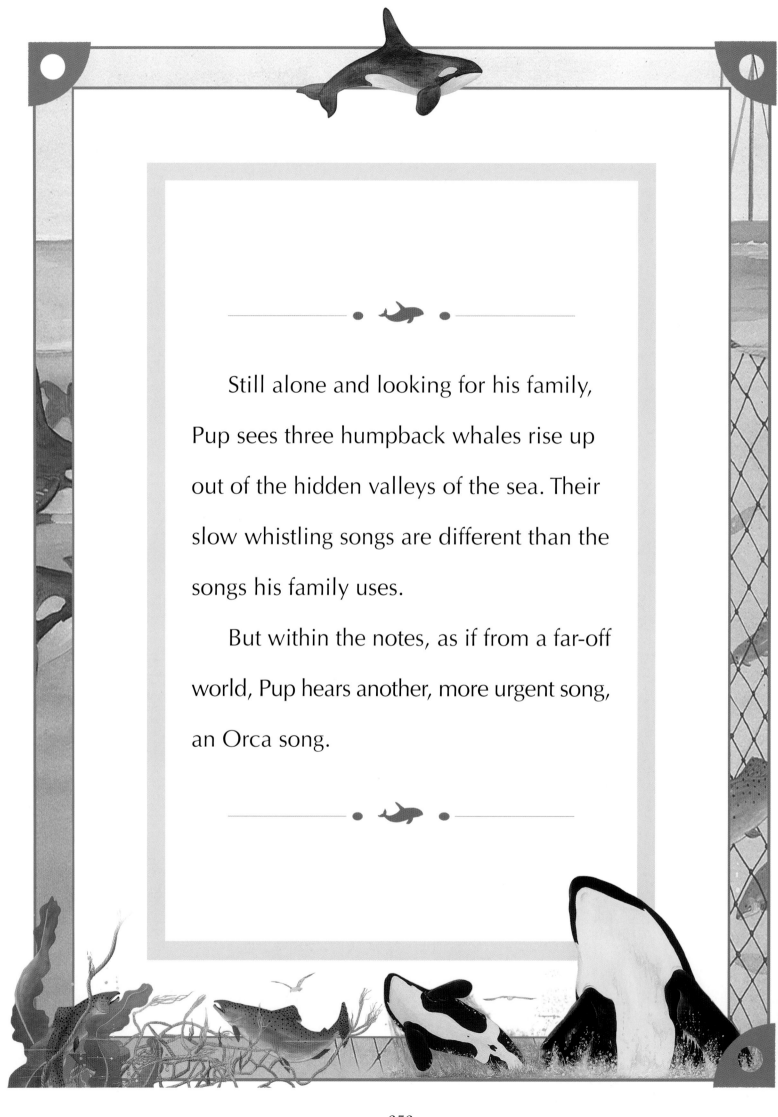

Still alone and looking for his family, Pup sees three humpback whales rise up out of the hidden valleys of the sea. Their slow whistling songs are different than the songs his family uses.

But within the notes, as if from a far-off world, Pup hears another, more urgent song, an Orca song.

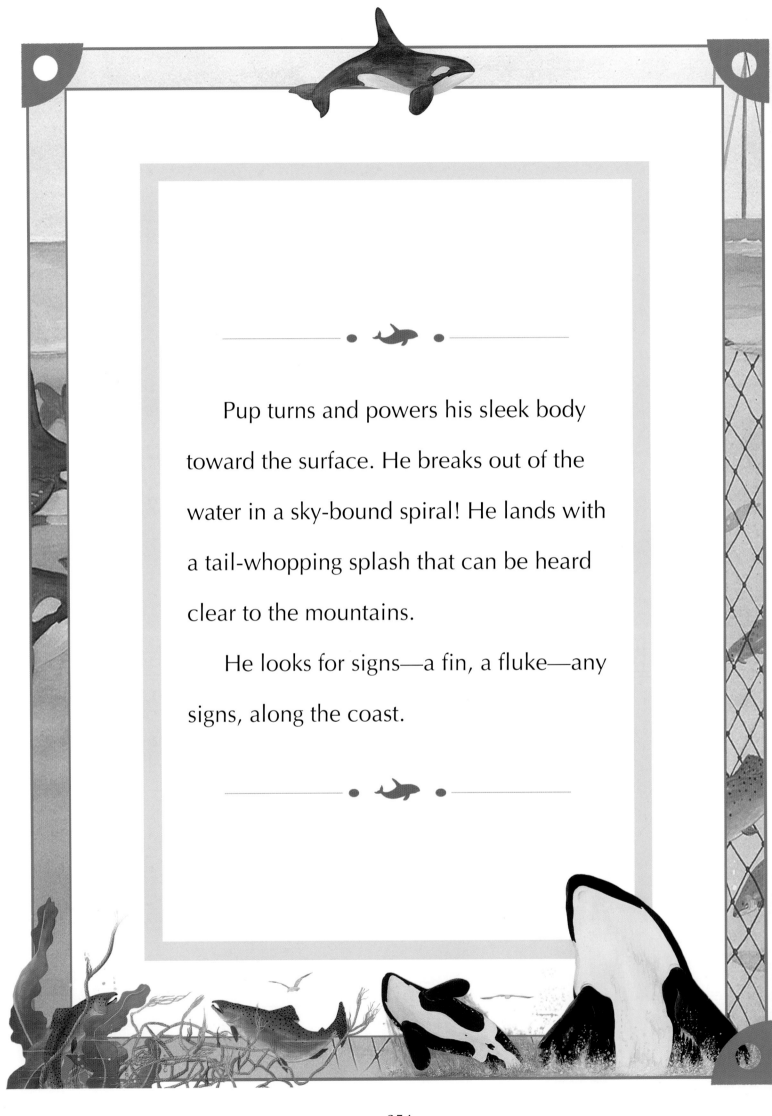

Pup turns and powers his sleek body toward the surface. He breaks out of the water in a sky-bound spiral! He lands with a tail-whopping splash that can be heard clear to the mountains.

He looks for signs—a fin, a fluke—any signs, along the coast.

And then, silhouetted against the sunset, Pup sees them—seven whales, his very own family, rising out of the waves, coming for him. They have not left him! They have come back!

Their songs of happiness race before them like ribbons of joy. Orca Pup is home again.